For You

Andreas Seidl

Handover of Power

Global Version

Volume 4: State Organisation

Imprint

Bibliographic information of the German National Library:
The German National Library lists this publication in the
German National Bibliography; detailed bibliographic data
are available on the Internet at http://dnb.dnb.de.

© 2022 Dipl. Pol. Theodor Andreas Seidl

Cover: Christiane Ebrecht
Translation: DeepL, Cologne
Production and publishing: BoD – Books on Demand,
Norderstedt

ISBN: 978-3-7568-1334-6

Acknowledgements

My thanks go to my family and friends who have made me who I am today. Special thanks to all those who supported me in writing this book. I would like to thank all my classmates, teachers, fellow students, lecturers, demonstrators, activists, colleagues, companies and countries with whom I have had the privilege of sharing the experiences from which all the ideas in this book have emerged. I would like to thank the staff of Books on Demand for their kind helpfulness. I thank the citizens of Seligenstadt for the harmony and solidarity in which I was able to write.

Foreword

This policy concept contains a variety of proposals for possible political reforms. It can be peacefully and democratically adapted to any current political system of any state in the world, but also to political systems in families, clubs, associations or companies. Wherever humans make or submit to rules that manage living together, the following proposals can be helpful. Readers who find the proposals so helpful that they would like to implement them together with like-minded people can contact the author. The contact form on the last page can be used for this purpose.

Faults and defects

I ask for your understanding that this volume was not professionally proofread. I could only afford professional proofreading for the summary. Spelling errors and unfortunate phrasing may therefore occur. As soon as this volume has sold enough to pay for a professional proofreading, it will be done. After that, a new edition will be published.

English version

Please understand that this volume has been translated automatically. I could only afford a professional translation for the summary. Poor wording and spelling errors may therefore occur. In case of doubt, the German version shall prevail. As soon as this volume has sold enough to pay for a professional translation, it will be done. After that, a new edition will be published. It was more important to me that no one in the world should have an information advantage than individual translation errors in the complete work.

References

If something has been quoted directly, it is set in italics. If the headings contain footnotes, the sources for direct and indirect quotations apply in the chapter for which the heading stands. Otherwise, quotations or source references are directly at the word or at the end of the sentence or paragraph. This book contains parts of text based on the Federal Constitution of the Swiss Confederation of 18 April 1999 (as of 12 February 2017), abbreviated to BV[1] and the Constitution of the Canton of Bern of 6 June 1993 (as of 11 March 2015), abbreviated to KV[2] .

If the constitutional paragraph, or individual paragraphs thereof, are based in whole or in part on extracts from the BV or KV, this is indicated in a footnote. The references to the corresponding footnotes for constitutional paragraphs are usually found after the heading of the affected chapter and sometimes in the body of the text. Articles used in the Swiss constitutions are listed in the footnote with a number after the title of the constitutional paragraph. Example: §123 Sample title: BV Art.123, KV Art.123.

All internet sources are fully cited in the footnotes. They were last accessed on 30.09.2021. All literature sources are also listed in full in the footnotes.

All references to tasks undertaken by other ministries and described in more detail there are given in footnotes. Example: Model Ministry - 1.2.3 Model Chapter.

All footnotes are to be viewed in comparison to the respective source, so-called indirect quotations. Direct quotations are set in italics, but hardly ever occur. The source reference is intended to enable further investigation and to take copyright

---

1 This is not an official publication. Only the publication by the Swiss Federal Chancellery is authoritative. https://www.fedlex.admin.ch/eli/cc/1999/404/de On 14.12.2021
2 This is not an official publication. The Bernese Official Collection of Laws is authoritative. https://www.belex.sites.be.ch/frontend/versions/2420?locale=de#ART71 On 16.12.2021

into account.

Table of contents

1 Goals of the Ministry of State Organisation

The aim of the Ministry of State Organisation is to organise the state with its ministries in such a way that the political structures and processes comply with the constitution and to serve as a contact and moderator for citizens and politicians. The objective of the Ministry of State Organisation is considered to have been achieved when the state apparatus functions in the interests of the citizens and for the benefit of the people.

The ministry ensures that the theory of the state follows coherent and comprehensible theses. The theories are to serve as directives for the practical implementation of the state organs. From this, concrete goals are derived that the state system and the governments should fulfil.

In order not to give too much power to any one organ of the state, the separation of powers is regulated. In order to give each political level the responsibility for which it is suited, subsidiarity is regulated. In order to describe all political levels and define their tasks, federalism is regulated. The political structure describes all state organs and how they interact in political processes to ensure the stability of the dynamic media democracy at all times.

2 Departments

The departments are divided into sub-departments and enumerations are usually considered as their individual units. Many tasks of some departments are completely taken over by other ministries as a service.

2.1 Central Department

Part of the Central Department is the Reception Office with the Courier and Mail Room, which directs all concerns, broadcasts and visitors to the appropriate place in the ministry.

2.1.1 Staff

The Human Resources Department is responsible for staff development and planning. For this purpose, it takes care of the recruitment of junior staff, intern and trainee programmes as well as the selection procedures for employees and special selection procedures for applicants with disabilities. For politicians and employees, the department prepares a job plan. In all its tasks, it works in voting with the personnel board.

All other personnel matters are transferred to the relevant ministries. The Ministry of Education is responsible for the training and further education of employees for the state service.[1] The Ministry of Labour takes over the service law.[2] This includes labour and collective bargaining law for employees in the state service, remuneration, personnel administration of all careers and employees, flexitime, holiday and sick leave, working time with or without flexitime in part-time or full-time at the place of work or in home work. The Ministry of Infrastructure provides housing assistance for all state employees.[3] The Ministry of Finance's Pay Office takes care of employees' salary, expenses, travel and relocation costs.[4] The Ministry of Education provides childcare for all employees in the state service.[5]

The Ministry of Health is responsible for the occupational health service.[6] It ensures occupational health management, deals with the treatment, education and prevention of occupational accidents, controls and provides occupational health and safety through the health auditors[7] of the Company Auditing Agency[8] .

---

1 Ministry of Education - 2.1.1.1 Education and training for the state service
2 Ministry of Labour - 4 State enterprises, 13 Labour Directory
3 Ministry of Infrastructure - 2.1.1.1 Housing assistance for state service employees
4 Ministry of Finance - 2.1.1.1 Staff remuneration
5 Ministry of Education - 2.1.1.2 Childcare for state service employees
6 Ministry of Health - 2.1.1.1 Occupational Health Service
7 Ministry of Labour - 20.7.2 Health auditor
8 Ministry of Labor - 20 Company Auditing Agency

2.1.1.1 Personnel board

The personnel board consists of all employees of the ministry. The personnel board meets whenever the HR department wants to reschedule, retrain, hire or dismiss personnel. Employees who are directly and indirectly affected by a personnel decision are given voting rights on the personnel board for that individual decision. The personnel board uses the procedures of direct, indirect and representative democracy for its projects. Meetings are held like committees. Each member can lend out his or her vote to another member and take it back. Working groups or staffs of entire agencies can elect leaders directly or rotate them to give them their vote. A vote cast may be reclaimed by a participation quorum. A leader can be newly elected by a deselection quorum. These two quorums can then only be voted for by those eligible to vote in the ministry's staff.

2.1.2 Organisation

The ministries of media, security, justice, finance, labour, state organisation provide audit services for quality management in the ministry, evaluation of work performance, revenues and expenditures, as well as corruption prevention, sabotage protection and, if necessary, disciplinary matters.[9]
The language service for translating talks or texts is provided by the Ministry of Education.[10] The Ministry of Finance organises the annual budget vote and ensures proper accounting in each ministry.[11] It regulates budget procedures, budget law, staff budgets, departmental budgets, costs and cash management, and assists ministries in budget planning for the budget vote. The Ministry of Labour regulates public procurement law and ensures corruption-free state orders and procurement.[12]
The Ministry of Digital Affairs supports the supply of

9Ministries of Media, Security, Justice, Finance, State Organisation - 2.1.2.1 Audit services
10Ministry of Education - 2.1.3 Language Service
11Ministry of Finance - 8 state revenues, 9 state expenditure
12Ministry of Labour - 6 Procurement Office

Information Technology.[13] In voting with the Procurement Office of the Ministry of Labour, it takes care of the procurement, provision, maintenance and service of technical devices and software. Much of this is produced in-house to ensure data protection in information and communication technology. Information technology and digitalisation officers audit and advise the ministries. Digital appointment calendar and documentation services are provided as well as a digital policy archive including a library.

2.1.2.1 Audit services

The Ministry of State Organisation provides quality management through the Federal Moderator's Office, which evaluates and organises the cooperation between the ministries and the citizens. The results of the evaluation are collected by the auditors of the Company Auditing Agency and Surveillance Television[14] and published on the intranet site of the Federal Moderator's Office.

The Guardians of the Constitution monitor state enterprises and authorities to ensure that the state adheres to the Constitution. The Guardians of the Constitution work with the Federal Moderator's Office and the Company Auditing Agency.

Prevention of corruption and protection against sabotage is regulated in the chapter on state security. To prevent corruption, government personnel can be reported to several agencies and are vetted by the Company Auditing Agency and the Surveillance Television[15] . Corrupt politicians can be removed from office directly through the deselection quorum. This is regulated in the chapter on Corruption and Crime in the State. To protect against sabotage, the population can take control of entire ministries or individual departments and units. This is regulated in the chapter on popular empowerment. Disciplinary matters are regulated in

---

13 Ministry of Digital Affairs - 2.1.2.1.1 Supply of Information Technology
14 Ministry of Media Affairs - 12.1 Monitoring team
15 Ministry of Media - 12 Surveillance Television

the subsection Sanctions. Violations can be reported on the intranet portal "Open Leaks", investigated in the committee of enquiry and punished by new elections, degradation and disempowerment.

2.2 Management Department

The Management Department is the minister's department. With his office team, he provides policy planning and analysis for his ministry and coordinates the relationship between the nation and the municipality through exchanges with his deputies in the municipalities. He initiates cooperation with other ministries or citizens in committees and is supported by the Ministry of State Organisation.

The Ministry of Media Affairs, through its media service, provides press and public relations for the ministry, moderates civil dialogue, trains or provides a spokesperson for the minister, writes speeches and texts on request, and ensures the implementation of conferences and events.[16]

The Ministry of Digital Affairs is responsible for digital management and thus provides departmental management. It automatically produces business statistics, staff surveys and the current state of research through statistics. It automatically forwards proposals to the affected or empowered state employees. In document management, it ensures digitalisation and that ministries share forms with each other.[17]

2.2.1 Planning and strategy

The policy planning of the ministry is described in the chapter Tasks of the Ministry. The policy analysis is limited to the elections, voting and committees. The Ministry of State Organisation is responsible for coordinating the ministries of media and digital affairs in such a way that the dates for elections of persons, committees and voting do not overlap and open a window of opportunity for citizens to inform

---

16 Ministry of Media Affairs - 2.2.1.1 Media Service
17 Ministry of Digital Affairs - 2.1.2.1 Digital Service

themselves and participate. An analysis evaluates the processes on the basis of the collected empirical values that users, citizens and politicians express in contributions or ratings. An analysis of the relationship between time and resources invested is produced and published in the course of the budget vote. Employees of the Ministry of State Organisation are responsible for carrying out the analysis in the Company Auditing Agency team and collect the data as part of the annual audit by the Company Auditing Agency.

The relationship between nations, nation and municipality is regulated in the chapters on cooperation procedures, state procedural law, subsidiarity and federalism.

Cooperation with other ministries or citizens in committees, is regulated in the chapters Federal Moderator's Office, Committees and Direct Legislation. The coordination of ministries by the Ministry of State Organisation is regulated in the chapters Federal Moderator's Office and Cooperation Procedures.

2.3 State Department

The State Department is responsible for compliance with state law and, in cooperation with the Minister of State Organisation, for the formulation of innovations in state law. It oversees the work of the Guardians of the Constitution, the Federal Moderator's Office and the Liability Insurance Fund. It ensures the operation of the State Directory[18] and Persons Directory and cooperation with the other ministries. It pays attention to the realisation of the objectives, theories and separation of powers in the dynamic media democracy.

2.4 State Structure Department

The State Structure Department ensures that state institutions perform all their functions in accordance with the constitution. It oversees that nationals are granted their rights in town halls and on the intranet, that politicians in their ministries

---

18Ministry of Digital - 12 Directories

act heterarchically for the benefit of the people, that political parties can carry out their programme work, government work and opposition work constitutionally with adequate resources, and that councils are involved in proceedings wherever necessary. The State Structure Department supports the state institutions in organising meetings and their moderation. In cooperation with the State Organisation Minister, deficiencies in the state structure can be remedied through innovations and introduced into the legislative process.

2.5 State Process Department

The State Process Department oversees compliance with procedural rules in all ordinary and extraordinary cases. It ensures the operation of the Quorum Directory, Committee Directory, Legislative Directory, Lobby Directory and Petition Directory. Keeps track of all ongoing and triggered quorums and oversees the proper execution of all subsequent proceedings. It oversees the granting of political rights and the right to vote to those entitled to vote and provides the election officer for this purpose. It is responsible for all forms of voting, whether direct, indirect or representative. In particular, it ensures that all votes are held that are mandatory.

It ensures budget votes in cooperation with the Ministry of Finance and real and digital events for committees in cooperation with the Ministries of Media and Digital. It oversees the direct, indirect or representative procedures of governments, legislation and election of persons. It is responsible, in cooperation with the Minister of State Organisation, for the procedures for constitutional amendments and in extraordinary situations where state security is at risk.

2.6 Subsidiarity Department

The Subsidiarity Department coordinates the federal distribution of responsibilities. It maintains contact with all political levels and keeps track of all the different areas of application of laws and the responsible politicians. It supervises the work of the Subsidiarity Agency and the subsidiarity votes. It supports the respective political level in complying with all special procedural rules in municipal, national or international procedures. In cooperation with the Ministry of Foreign Affairs, it coordinates efforts or refusals for international communitarisation. In cooperation with the Council of Ministers, municipal party councils, municipalities governed by municipalities, alliances of municipalities or cultural protection areas, the Subsidiarity Department organises the balance between international and national unity and municipal self-government.

2.7 Switching Department

The Switching Department organises the switch to the new system in all ministries. It drives the amendment of the constitution and all subsequent adjustments by other ministries and in codes. It coordinates all moves and changes of use of state buildings and capital city locations. It carries out retraining, dismissals and new appointments. Once the switch to the new system is completed in all ministries and the new constitution is in force, the Switching Department is closed.

3 Tasks of the Ministry of State Organisation

The task of the Ministry of State Organisation is to organise the state with its political structures and processes so that all state power emanates from the people. It is fulfilled in that the political structures and processes adapt flexibly to the population's dynamic willingness to participate. This ranges from representative and indirect procedures in councils when voter turnout is too low, to direct participation of the citizens in committees, voting in individual cases or permanently, to taking over entire ministries or the defence of state security.

The central task of the Ministry of State Organisation is to legislate for the procedures of election of persons, government, legislation and constitution-making. All citizens, politicians, parties and ministries that have to manage these procedures are accompanied and supported by the Federal Moderator's Office. The Ministry of State Organisation uses quorums as a central steering element. With the exception of the periodic budget vote, they are the driving forces behind the political processes. They are followed by negotiations in committees or councils and voting in polling stations or councils.

The everyday task of the Federal Moderator's Office is to ensure cooperation between the ministries and between the state and the citizens in accordance with the constitution. For the division of responsibilities between the municipal, national and international levels, the ministry maintains the Subsidiarity Agency. The State Directory provides an overview of all organs of the state and enables contact and communication between all participants. In particular, the Ministry of State Organisation is responsible for providing opportunities for citizens to participate and for guaranteeing election and voting rights.

As guardians of the Constitution, the Minister of State Organisation and his deputies are charged with ensuring compliance with the Constitution and with reporting and preventing violations. They are supported in this by the Guardians of the Constitution. In order to prevent dangers to state security, the Ministry of State Organisation ensures that the necessary procedures are followed and practised by the population.

The Ministry of State Organisation regulates the transition of the current state system to the new system described in this volume, the Constitution and the other volumes.

4 State law[19]

The Ministry of State Organisation is responsible for state law, i.e. the political processes and structures in the country. Political processes are quorums and the procedures of committees, elections of persons and legislation. Political structures are ministries, parties, committees, councils and the constitution. Since state law affects all ministries, it must be fundamentally laid down in the constitution. More concrete formulations in

---

19§247,1-3 State law

state organisation law are made by laws of the Ministry of State Organisation. State organisation law regulates the observance and reorganisation of the applicable structures and processes so that political contents can be devised and implemented.
All 18 ministers are involved in the legislative process for state law. The text of the law must be negotiated in a committee or council. State law forms the basis for the administrative law procedures in the ministries and parties from which state services arise. State law consists of laws that oblige state agencies or citizens to act or enable them to act. The Ministry of Justice legislates on the jurisprudence in state law.[20] The Ministry of State Organisation describes why the state procedures are necessary in the applicable state law in state theories.

4.1 State procedural law[21]

The Ministry of State Organisation ensures smooth cooperation between ministries, political levels and the state and its citizens. Cooperation is always necessary when several ministries or levels are affected by a project. The procedures are laid down in the State Procedural Law. The political contents constitute the individual cases of political decisions made within the applicable political structure and through applicable political processes. Citizens, elected ministers, elected ministry staff and party members are responsible for political contents. In individual cases, they may involve several remits and require humans to work together who have never or rarely worked together before. The Ministry of State Organisation uses state procedural law to promote cooperation through moderation and uniform procedures. The authorities responsible for this are the Federal Moderator's Office and the Subsidiarity Agency. If conflicts of jurisdiction arise between ministries or authorities, the Subsidiarity Agency investigates the case, attempts to mediate or sends moderators. If no solution enters, the Minister of State Organisation makes the decision or it is negotiated in a committee and then voted on.

---

20 Ministry of Justice - 4.8.3 State law
21 §46,1,2 State, §114,5 Federal Moderator's Office: BV Art.157, §111,5 Administration, §247,3 State law

4.1.1 Lack of responsibility[22]

If the entrance occurs that no ministry feels responsible for a case, but the state has the mandate to act, the Ministry of State Organisation takes over the legislative process and the execution of these laws in this case until it assigns the corresponding responsibility to a ministry or a new ministry is created.

4.1.2 Establishment and closure of ministries[23]

The people can establish a new ministry by introducing an initiative for this purpose, which must be approved by the people with a majority of 75% or more. Since the constitution must be amended when a new ministry is established, all procedures are treated as a partial revision of the constitution. If the initiative is introduced as a draft, the government programme for the new ministry is created in a committee. If the initiative is introduced as a template, it is voted on immediately. Counter-drafts may be submitted. The procedure otherwise corresponds to the election of persons process, in which a candidates' committee follows. For the new remit, the new party begins its work and forms party wings.
The Ministry of State Organisation can close ministries or assign responsibilities to another ministry or divide them between several ministries. For each of these operations, all ministers and 75% of the citizens must agree. If a majority is not reached, a committee is convened, after which another voting follows. The ministers are then entitled to vote only as citizens. If 65% of the citizens vote in favour, the operation is carried out.

4.1.3 Communication

The ministries of state organisation, media and digital affairs create a communication system through which citizens are able to manage the state. The Ministry of State Organisation

---

22§46.6 State: BV Art.173
23§99.5-7 Ministries

sets the rules of procedure for how the Ministries of Media and Digital Affairs provide the necessary communication technology and how they may use it. The Ministry of Media Affairs provides for time-saving information intake through filming and enables cooperation between viewers and performers through different formats. The Ministry of Digital Affairs provides networking and equipment with up-to-date software and hardware through which communication activities can be carried out and archived.

4.1.4 National language[24]

The national language is the language spoken by most nationals. All official business must be available to nationals in at least the national language. If states with different languages are communitarised, a new language must be developed that can contain words from all national languages. The Ministry of Integration is responsible for the official languages.[25]

4.1.5 National anthem

The national anthem is a song whose melody and lyrics are voted on by the people, like a law. Therefore, it is listed in the Law Directory as a law of the Ministry of State Organisation. Once the repeal quorum is reached, amendments are negotiated in a People's Committee. A competition may be announced for which domestic musicians may submit proposals. The people vote on the negotiated amendments.

4.2 Cooperation processes[26]

The Ministry of State Organisation is responsible for cooperation in three cooperation processes.
The first cooperation process serves to ensure that the municipal, national and international levels cooperate with

---

24 §53 National language, §185 Languages: BV Art.70
25 Ministry of Integration - 6.1 Official languages
26 §108.5 Composition and election of the government

each other or clearly separate their responsibilities.

The second cooperation process serves to ensure that the four economic zones remain permeable so that nationals can decide at any time in which economic zone they would like to work or live. The Ministry of Labour assumes primary responsibility there, but is supported by the Ministry of State Organisation. The third cooperation process serves to enable ministries to offer solutions that only several ministries can manage together and no ministry alone. The Ministry of State Organisation checks whether reports by ruling or presumably affected ministers or by citizens are admissible by veto quorum. Reports are admissible if the law-making provision affected exceeds the departmental scope of a ministry. Then it is examined which of the 18 ministries are affected. The reasons given in the reports are taken into account. After a report has been examined and approved, the ministers of all affected ministries are involved in the legislative process. The Federal Moderator's Office acts as the leader.

4.3 State Organisation Minister

The national Minister of State Organisation is responsible for monitoring whether the country's constitution has been respected. This task cannot be shifted to the international or municipal level through a subsidiarity vote. In order to carry out this task, the Minister of State Organisation, in voting with the judges of the Constitutional Court, may give direct instructions to all state employees or veto laws. These laws must then be brought into line with the constitution or repealed. To assist the Minister of State Organisation in this task, the Ministry of State Organisation maintains a Department of Guardians of the Constitution.

4.3.1 Guardians of the Constitution

The Ministry of State Organisation is responsible for ensuring that political institutions abide by the constitution and act only within its constitutionally prescribed limits. Constitutional disputes are reported to the Guardians of the Constitution or identified by the Guardians themselves, and are heard and resolved in a committee away from court proceedings. The Guardians of the Constitution provide oversight of state enterprises and authorities through cooperation with auditors from the Company Auditing Agency[27] , the Federal Moderator's Office, the police and the Constitutional Court. Citizens can report doubts about the constitutionality of actions of citizens, companies, civil or state organisations to the police[28] . The police have the duty to examine the doubts and then immediately report them to the Constitutional Court.[29]

At the Federal Moderator's Office, citizens and politicians can voice complaints about state agencies. It is checked whether laws or the constitution are being violated. The moderators report the findings to the affected state agencies and set a deadline of 3 months for the violations to be remedied. If the deadline passes without the violations being remedied, the Federal Moderator's Office reports the matter to the Constitutional Court.

If legality auditors discover violations during the Company Auditing Agency's annual audit, they must be remedied within 3 months. If this is not the case, the matter is reported to the Constitutional Court.

The Constitutional Court is obliged to carry out a legal examination of all reported cases and, if violations are found, to initiate proceedings. The Constitutional Court hears reported violations of the constitution and can impose sentences or propose amendments to legislation.

4.3.2 Fundamental rights

The fundamental rights are laid down by the people in the constitution in the chapter on fundamental rights. Different ministries are responsible for the implementation of individual articles of the fundamental rights. Compliance

27 Ministry of Labour - 20.7.3 Economic auditor
28 Ministry of Security - 7 Police
29 Ministry of Justice - 5.4.6 Constitutional Court

with fundamental rights is evaluated by the Guardians of the Constitution and the distribution of responsibilities is moderated by the Federal Moderator's Office.

4.4 Federal Moderator's Office[30]

The Ministry of State Organisation maintains the Federal Moderator's Office. The office is an independent agency in which Federal Moderators, as directly elected politicians, are accountable to the laws and citizens. The special duty of Federal Moderators is to conduct negotiations in a neutral manner. This means that no interest goes unmentioned, there must be no taboos based on supposed political correctness, all criticism must be examined for its cause, no ministry is valued more than another or several, and no distinction must be made between citizens on the basis of their status.
The ministers and their deputies elect a Federal Moderator as State Moderator, who becomes Chief of Internal Service. The citizens elect a Federal Moderator as Citizen Moderator who becomes Chief of External Service.

4.4.1 Internal Service[31]

The Internal Service is the staff unit for all governments that require a leader to moderate the cooperation of several ministries, levels or authorities. Moderation can be used in legislation, the legislature, and execution, the executive. In this Internal Service, the Federal Moderator's Office provides moderation between state agencies. There are Federal Moderators for the municipal and national levels. Moderators at the international level are the representatives or ambassadors of the Ministry of Foreign Affairs.[32] They receive additional training in the Internal Service.
The Internal Service is also responsible for the training of new Federal Moderators. Federal Moderators for the discussion

30§46.2 State, §114 Federal Moderator's Office: KV Art.96, BV Art.157, §113,9 Media Democracy
31§114,1,5 Federal Moderator's Office: BV Art.179, BV Art.157
32Ministry of Foreign Affairs - 4.7 Embassies

rounds in committees and councils are trained here. If the concept of Solution Finders[33] is used, the voting moderator is trained in the Ministry of Digital Affairs and the audience moderator in the Ministry of Media Affairs. Once the training is completed, the moderators can stand for election as municipal or national Federal Moderators.

4.4.2 External Service[34]

The External Service provides moderation of communication between citizens and state agencies. It receives all statements from citizens that citizens wish to address to a state agency. This refers to all the possibilities available to citizens through their political rights. Citizens do not need to know the details of these rights. The External Service maintains an ombudsman's office for citizens in every town hall. Here they learn which state agencies are most suitable for asserting citizens' interests. Citizens are presented with all possible procedures. In this way, the Federal Moderator's Office contributes to the political education of the citizens. The election of which procedure is to be used is up to the citizen. As advice, assessments can be made on the prospects of success based on past similar cases. The statistical result of all possible procedures is calculated by the Algoracle[35] and given to the citizen along with the personal assessment of the staff member of the ombudsman's office.

4.4.2.1 Citizens' consultation hours

The ombudsman's office is also the contact for citizens who want to go to a politician's consulting hour. Every politician has his or her office hours for citizens at least one working day per week. These consulting hours have open and appointment-based consulting hours. When making an appointment, it is also possible to indicate whether the consulting hour will be held via People's Computer. While no citizens are present, the

---

33 Ministry of Media Affairs - 7.2.3.5 Solution Finder (Legislation Committee)
34 §114.4 Federal Moderator's Office
35 Ministry of Digital Affairs - 15.3 Algoracle

politician is involved in the discussions in the user community on the intranet. Lobbyists are not allowed to use the citizens' consultation hours. If they do, the meeting must be filmed in real time and published.[36]

4.4.3 Federal Moderators[37]

Federal Moderators are considered directly elected politicians of the Ministry of State Organisation and have their own deselection quorum. They chair committees and councils. This means that they organise and moderate the events, including preparation and follow-up. They work regularly on state television as news anchors and show moderators. On the intranet, they accompany discussion rounds, stop hostilities and look for common ground and compromises.

4.4.4 Two presiding Federal Moderators

The first Federal Moderator anchors the news on Government Television[38] and is the people's ombudsman. Complaints and proposals sent to him should first be sent to the relevant state agencies responsible for the matter in the complaint. If an agreement is reached, the case is closed. If there is no agreement, the complaint is reported in the news to give citizens a chance to report similar cases, find a majority for the case and force action by the ministry by quorum. This Federal Moderator heads the External Service of the Federal Moderator's Office.

The second Federal Moderator moderates the Solution Finder shows[39] and is responsible for coordinating among ministries when ministries are tackling a project together. Ministers, but also all other state employees, can turn to him. Thus, the second Federal Moderator is more or less the ombudsman for state employees. His goal is to avoid at all times that

---

36 Ministry of Media Affairs - 7.2.1.3 Lobby documentation
37 §115 Moderators
38 Ministry of Media - 7 Government Television
39 Ministry of Media Affairs - 7.2.3.5 Solution Finder (Legislation Committee)

no one feels responsible for anything or that several state employees feel responsible and thus confuse the citizens. This Federal Moderator heads the Internal Service of the Federal Moderator's Office.

4.4.4.1 Stalemate

The Federal Moderator mediates between ministries. However, if two or more ministries still cannot agree, the Federal Moderator of the Internal Service decides. This process must be reported in the news on state television. Citizens can punish the provocateur of a stalemate by its deselection quorum.

4.4.4.2 Hotline

Citizens can call an External Service telephone centre to find out how to complain about something, make a suggestion for improvement or which elected state employees are responsible for something and where it is possible to put the vote in the deselection quorum. The first Federal Moderator is responsible for this hotline. Citizens do not have to call, they can also submit their concerns in writing or by video via the State Directory on the intranet site of the first Federal Moderator.

4.5 State Directory

In the State Directory, all ministries and parties have a profile where they can present all information about their work and organisational structure and indicate voting and links. The profiles are their websites on the intranet. In groups, ministries make their departments, units and authorities accessible, parties their wings and working groups.
Via the profile, citizens can see in the organisation chart which politician or party wing leaders are responsible for a decision or execution. A link takes users directly to the appropriate quorum in the Quorum Directory.

4.6 Persons Directory

The Persons Directory is part of the registration system and is maintained by the Residents' Registration Office.[40] All personal data, such as name, age, height, hair and eye colour, place of birth, place of residence, date of birth, gender and last change date are stored in the Persons Directory profile. Profiles can form groups for common interests and circles of friends.

All data of a citizen is considered his or her property. The state has the right to collect and analyse this data. At the same time, the state also has the duty of confidentiality towards third parties who are not in the state service. All access to the data must be recorded in the access log.[41] Exceptions are only permitted for criminal prosecution until the judgement becomes final. After that, all state accesses appear in the logs. Citizens themselves have the right to disclose their data to other humans and to publish more or less personal data about themselves. Each user defines the group of persons himself.[42] This can serve the purpose of finding partners for business, relationships or living situations.

The Persons Directory contains the most important data that establishes and verifies the identity of a human being and also guarantees this identity verification in the digital world of the intranet. Identity verification is indispensable for the conclusion of contracts in accordance with the rule of law. Treaties via the intranet are thus particularly safeguarded because anonymity is contrary to contract law.

All other profiles of other directories access the data set of the Persons Directory to check the identity of a user. In this way, "social bots" can be avoided. Every action on the intranet can be assigned to a user. The Persons Directory serves as a central interface for all directories, so that all personal data created about a user in other directories or files is also available in the profile of the Persons Directory.

---

40 Ministry of Integration - 4.4 Residents' Registration Office
41 Ministry of Digital Affairs - 7.5 Access Directory
42 Ministry of Digital Affairs - 7 Digital data protection

4.6.1 Expression of interest

On the profile page of the users in the Persons Directory there is a field: "Expression of interest". Here you should indicate what you would like to do with other humans. You are given a choice of different categories and can create new sub-items yourself. This should make it easy for humans to find something to do together without knowing each other. You can activate the radius search or search nationwide. Rare interests that are difficult to find can still be shared.

4.7 Liability insurance

The Ministry of State Organisation operates a liability insurance scheme for all state employees. Employees in the state service and politicians can take out insurance against negligent faults in office. The premium amount is measured by how much damage all policyholders cause and recover through insurance premiums. Covered are damages that are prosecuted under civil law and do not exceed a damage amount of 10 billion Dollars.

5 Theories of dynamic media democracy

Dynamic media democracy is based on various theories of coexistence and its management. Theories are useful to plan concrete implementations on their basis or to adapt common implementations to the level of development of humanity.

The following describes how the political processes and structures interlock and result in citizens holding state powers in their hands and being able to lend out or relinquish as much of them as they wish.

Citizens can communicate directly with each other and the state via the intranet and state television. If there are enough interested and motivated citizens among the people, the government of the country can be done by its citizens in a division of labour. Every citizen has expertise in at least one of the 18 ministries. Citizens group themselves online and offline into *parties* with local chapters and party wings. The 18 capital cities are home to the 18 party headquarters.

Ministers are elected state employees who take responsibility for one of the 18 ministries. Citizens can access all staff of all ministries for committees to obtain expertise for legislative or review processes from the specialist departments of the 18 ministries. Citizens check on the work of ministries via the intranet and state television. Citizens can dismiss and re-select all staff of all ministries by popular empowerment in case of emergency.

Councils are service providers. Citizens cast their vote to councils of ministers when a majority of 65% decides in a participation quorum not to continuously vote in favour of each law of one or more ministries. Members of councils of ministers have a deselection quorum. Each vote by all members of a council is documented in a graph. If a member of parliament does not vote in the sense of his or her constituents, each individual citizen can contribute to the deselection of that member of parliament.

Insofar as citizens have lent out their vote and yet vote themselves, affected delegates to the party caucus lose that vote. Delegates always vote with all the votes they represent in all their votes. The voting results are given up to the fourth decimal place. In this way, all votes can be discussed and decided by citizens via their People's Computers at any time. An automatic measurement shows how much the citizens use the delegates or councils as service providers or not. If more and more citizens want to vote directly, the participation quorum is triggered.

5.1 Theory of collective consciousness through media

The dynamic media democracy is designed to enable masses of people to manage themselves and create a collective consciousness made visible through the media. Digitalisation allows humans to network worldwide through the internet via smartphone or computer. Actually, only the brains are networking, because the humans in front of the computers are mostly quiet and motionless. The self-motivated networking of human brains automatically creates a meta-level. On this meta-level lies the collective consciousness. The brains of individual citizens are like brain regions responsible for different tasks. The intranet provides a safe place for the state brain. The intranet symbolises the "superego" in human psychology. This is the part of us humans that always wants to follow rules so that everyone does well. The internet will never be shut down because it is the mother of the intranet. This is where the programmes and algorithms were invented and developed that make the intranet work in the first place. However, the internet will always offer a lawless space. In human psychology, the internet symbolises the "it". This is the part of us humans that wants to follow our drives, instincts and desires. Humanity, peoples, municipalities or groups are able to act together through the intranet. The acting people of the dynamic media democracy symbolise the "I". This is the part in us humans that we communicate to our environment as long as we live as acting humans. A collective consciousness is able to act inventively. This makes it quicker and easier to find solutions and innovations.

5.2 Theory of the social psychological adolescence of humanity

Humanity develops like humans, only with a time delay. Their life days are generations. Humans learn to walk and talk at about the same time, but usually one after the other. Mankind learned to walk from crawling to running between 1800 and 2000. First the railway, then the automobile and finally the aeroplane were made available to the masses. Today, humanity moves globally. In 2000, humanity began to learn to speak with the internet. Since then, humans have sometimes babbled meaningless stuff, sometimes coherent words over the social networks. Democracy today in 2022 is stuck on the infant age. Humans can either shout at demonstrations or draw a cross in a circle. Otherwise, politicians and the mass media just talk at them and present an environment regulated by others.

The dynamic media democracy provides the humans who use it with the vocabulary to speak. The media of the dynamic media democracy are the human language tools. The mouth is the People's Computer and the People's Committee, the lungs including the chest are the intranet and the throat with the vocal cords is the state television with all its content.

Humanity now has until 2200 to learn a unified mother tongue. It should be a self-confident language that chooses its grammar sensibly in order to be able to express itself as clearly as possible. This process must be moderated and accompanied so that it is successfully completed.

Educational psychology shows which developmental steps are still to come. The Oedipus complex and the defiance phase are examples of how the collective consciousness will behave during its development. Puberty could be the detachment process from Mother Earth and Father State, in which masses of people set out to colonise foreign planets.

As we all know, development takes time and many faults are made. Only when mistakes are learned from constructively can a healthy mind grow. Punishing faults is not expedient here. Masses of people will make faults. They need to be discussed so that cause and effect become clear. In the end, there should be a solution with which faults can be avoided. What is a fault and what is not is decided by the citizens of the dynamic media democracy themselves.

The long-term goal is to develop all the brains of humans into a meta-brain with its own consciousness. Humanity will then become a self-aware being that does not damage itself but discovers new worlds.

5.2.1 Theory of the social-psychological adolescence of peoples

Children growing up resembles the developmental steps of humanity. Humans learned to walk when trains, cars and aeroplanes made the whole world accessible to everyone. Humanity learned to see when cameras and televisions found their way into everyday life. Learned to hear when microphones and loudspeakers provided radio. Mankind is currently learning to speak through the internet and computers.

Cooperation is slowly becoming possible, but is still strongly reduced to satisfying one's own needs. The situation can be compared to toddlers who play together but can't say anything to each other. Their interaction simply brings them fun. It is similar with world trade. Every company tries to satisfy the needs of individuals. Companies that satisfy the needs of humanity do not yet exist because there are no clearly formulated needs.

Just as toddlers play with each other and fun immediately turns into seriousness when the other person claims ownership of their own toy or seat, so too peace turns into war when one country disputes the other country's property.

The individual human has the role of an organelle, an organisation such as a club or a company has the role of a cell. Institutions have the role of organs. The political structure is the skeleton of the bone, cameras are the eyes, microphones the ears, speakers the mouth and machines the hands. A product is usually produced by several cells together.

The role of the child falls to a people. The role of the parents falls to the governments. In the course of adolescence, the peoples reduce themselves to a world society and the governments to the will of the people. Every founding of a new state with its own people can be compared to the birth of a child when states are divided, i.e. when borders are drawn. Every unification of states, i.e. dissolution of borders, reduces the number of children to one child, which is on its way to becoming an adult. Figuratively speaking, the community of nations is currently a group of small children who can already walk and are just learning to speak. The more states unify, the fewer children are in this kindergarten group. At the end of the school career, only one pupil leaves this class. His or her personality carries the personalities of all classmates. The age of this human is measured in generations. A generation is one day in the life of humanity, assuming that all humans become parents at the age of 20 on average.

As a growing youth emancipates itself more and more from its parents, so the peoples become more and more democratic and the world society lives in a direct democracy. Humanity is initially represented by many childlike need-oriented personalities, but at the end of its adolescence it is an adult human being with a personality that has great understanding of all situations due to versatile experiences. This adult human being, who represents humanity in this theory, has four goals: First of all, he must keep healthy and take care of his household. Keeping healthy includes not allowing war, because that would be like a cancer that metastasises in the body through hatred. Fanatical religions or ideologies are like pathogens that infect the body. Taking care of the household means not destroying the earth and using resources in such a way that one is able to survive with them. Wasting resources could mean death from hunger, cold or heat.

Secondly, he wants to move out of his childhood home, Earth, and colonise new planets.

Thirdly, he wants to get to know other living beings in the universe and form partnerships with sympathetic beings.

Fourthly, it wants to ally itself with the partner that is most similar to it in such a way that, in the course of evolution, fertile offspring arise from this partnership in order to preserve the species. In this way, humanity can colonise planets together with extraterrestrials and together make new planets habitable or find them.

According to this theory, a future framework plan is derived, which is to be protected and advanced by the constitution. The goal is to gradually convince all humans to work together as an emancipated organism in order to be able to act in the universe as an independently survivable personality, be it for the prevention of danger from celestial bodies, planetary colonisation or communication with extraterrestrials.

5.3 Theory of the state as an entrepreneur in the national economy[43]

The Ministry of State Organisation ensures smooth workflows between ministries and democratic decision-making with the citizens. The comparable role to elections is the human resources department and to legislation is controlling. Parties handle marketing, the Ministry of Media Affairs handles advertising, information and PR (public relations).

---

43 §46.3 State

The decisive factor is the transparent presentation of all processes in which the state is involved, so that the people, as owners of the state, can monitor their "company". One could compare it to nationals being equally involved participants in their "state plc". Shares in the state plc are only issued to domestic nationals, one per person, namely the identity card. Upon death, the shareholder right of influence expires. Politicians are the managers. The shareholders jointly elect the managers, tell them exactly what they have to implement or how the "company" deals with customers. If the manager does not carry it out to their satisfaction, he is dismissed.

The company has at least one and a maximum of four part-time managers for each ministry.

Shareholder and customer are one person here, but the difference is that the shareholders only have a joint decision-making capacity, but the customer does not. He can make the decisions in his own life as long as he abides by the rules he has chosen with his people.

The state has a monopoly on legislation within its national borders. It exploits this profitably to raise the standard of living of its people.

The state actively and progressively manages profits in order to reduce taxes in the long term.

State services are offered by subscription through taxes or by unit price as fees.

The state as a monopolist creates different sales markets for itself, namely the four different economic forms. The citizens permanently engage in self-discrimination in the face of market power. The citizens as customers discriminate against themselves here by choosing how many state services they want and whether they want to pay for the services individually or have them available permanently and indefinitely as a Tax-funded service. They also signal their willingness to pay by their election of the economic form in which they consume, work and live.

The state uses the insights of economics and business administration to generate stable slight profit growth in the long term throughout the country, but at least in its state budget.

The state, as a potent company, ensures that savings are built up in order to be able to compensate for fluctuations in orders or economic fluctuations from its own resources.

The state may not borrow abroad if the termination of these debts could result in a state bankruptcy. Foreign debts may only be taken on after a referendum to offset People's Bank[44] losses to customers or their capital in order to close the current financial year. The following financial year must then manage with fewer benefits or with higher taxes.

The state sees other states as competitors and partners. In the short term, they are competitors who, on the stage of international anarchy without a state monopoly on the use of force, either annex national borders or wrest labour and customers away from them. In the medium term, international agreements regulate the free movement of citizens as workers and customers. In the long run, all states merge to create the natural monopoly of self-government of mankind. It is uneconomical to have several national governments because there is only one earth and one species of man. As long as there are states, there is a danger of negative externalities because states can enrich themselves at the expense of other states by polluting the environment there rather than taking advantage of the domestic environment or a lower standard of living in another country.

The state is a democratically run company in which the citizens are the employees and customers. The goal of management is to retain customers in the long term, who are becoming more and more solvent, and to retain employees who are increasingly better trained and constantly bring innovative ideas for new services. The management consists of the ministers, who are directly elected by their customers and employees, the citizens. The state resembles a corporation with many limited companies. The corporate management is the national government with its ministers and their ministries. The departments of the ministries are service-providing or producing limited liability

---

44Ministry of Finance - 11 People's Bank

companies. New limited companies can be founded for municipal self-administration.

5.4 Theory of short chains of legitimacy

The chain of legitimacy is the path from the will of the people to the execution of the will of the people by the state. In classical democratic policy, there is the separation of powers of the legislative, executive and judiciary. In the dynamic mediative democracy, the people have democratic control over all powers and there is also the fourth power, the mediative. As a service for the convenience of a population weary of voting, the dynamic media democracy offers councils that the citizens only put into service by a low voter turnout of less than 40% or by a participation quorum. Otherwise, the following chain of legitimacy applies:

Legislation

Domestic nationals directly elect all 18 ministers. In legislative processes, ministers must negotiate the content of a proposed law either with their ministry or in a People's Committee, or in a council. Committees are broadcast in real time on Government Television so that viewers can participate via their People's Computer .[45]

Laws and ministers have an unlimited repeal or deselection quorum. If nationals are dissatisfied with a law or minister, they force a review or a new election.

Behind the legislation are the 18 political parties and the citizens who offer new policy solutions.

Executive

Because all 18 ministers are directly elected, they can be held directly responsible for actions of their ministry. However, some ministries have mandatory elections for leaders in the ministry. For example, the presidents for Company Auditing Agency, People's Bank have to be directly elected and some have to be elected by municipalities. If the people discover leaders in the ministries who should be directly elected or no longer elected, a staff quorum can be triggered and a voting called at any time.

45 Ministry of Digital Affairs - 13.6 People's Computers

Judiciary

Not only the Minister of Justice is elected, but also all judges in the courts. Municipal Court judges are elected municipal by the affected population. All judges in other national courts, are elected by the people. International judges are elected by the peoples once international communitarisation has progressed to that point. The new election is by deselection quorum for which those entitled to vote are the affected population.

Mediative

The ministers for media and digital affairs are directly elected, but so are moderators, intendants and administrators. In addition, citizens can also create their own images, sounds and videos, which they publish on local or Nationwide Citizen Television or on the intranet.[46]

International

At the international level, the foreign minister is responsible for laws and politicians that originate outside the domestic sphere but have an effect on the population at home. For an International Union, at least two ministries from two member states must unify their laws and have an international minister elected directly by the peoples as soon as possible. Until then, municipal deputy ministers and national ministers in the International Council are responsible for the policies of the International Union.

6 Goals of the dynamic media democracy

There are three goals towards which the dynamic media democracy should lead the humans. The first goal is peace, first in one's own country, later on the whole earth. The second goal is an equal standard of living, first in one's own country, later on the whole earth. The third goal is to find and colonise new Earth-like planets.

46Ministry of Media - 9 Local Television, 11 Nationwide Citizen Television

6.1 Politics is a party

Dynamic media democracy is a policy in which the humans who make policy for and with each other also celebrate it together. Political events always include light shows, music, dance, drugs, drinks and food.

Light shows should fascinate humans and arouse their creativity and curiosity. Music should motivate humans to venture out of their homes and into the streets to participate in the policy event. Dance should strengthen the sense of community and create unity among the participants. Drugs are supposed to increase exuberance and also expand consciousness in humans who consume them. Through humans with expanded consciousness, the political discussion is enriched with new ideas and influences. Drinks, food and sanitary facilities should make it possible to stay longer at the political event and ensure a lasting sense of well-being.

6.2 Government goals

Ministers always set targets and minimum requirements. It is important that the common goal of the people is clear. The path to this goal includes many small intermediate goals. The ministers develop these intermediate goals and write the programme for them together with their party. The population can accept the programme, reject it or still change it by committee and then vote. For the achievement of intermediate goals, gifts are given to the people or celebrations are held. For example, electricity is free for one month a year.

7 Separation of powers[47]

The separation of powers serves the principle that no single person or group of persons may have sole control over the making of law, executive, judicial and mediating powers. The ministries are the state authorities that divide the powers among themselves and are controlled and influenced by the citizens. The state only takes on tasks that are given to it by the constitution and the laws. The citizens express their

---

47§69 Separation of powers: KV Art.66

will through the formulation of constitutional articles, laws, initiatives, petitions, programmes, as well as through quorums and voting.

The four powers consist firstly of the executive power, the executive. Execution is carried out by all employees of the ministries, who receive their tasks from the directly elected executives, deputy ministers and ministers. How the tasks are carried out is decided jointly by all members of the ministry in a heterarchical manner.

Secondly, there is the Law-making power, the legislation. Law-making is carried out by those entitled to vote through the election of persons and the legislative process. Citizens can get involved in these processes to a greater or lesser extent by triggering the participation quorum or the veto quorum and choosing one of three forms of participation by majority vote. If they want to be very involved, they choose direct democracy. If they want to participate strongly, they choose indirect democracy. If they want to participate weakly, they choose representative democracy. Those entitled to vote are citizens, international, national, municipal or deputy ministers, or party delegates, depending on the form of democracy.

Thirdly, there is the judicial power, the judiciary. The jurisprudence is carried out by directly elected judges in court proceedings. The judges judge according to the applicable law, which has been created by the legislation. The Ministry of Justice determines through legislative procedures who is involved in which court proceedings and with what task.

Fourthly, there is the mediating power, the mediative. The mediation of communication between ministries and between the state and citizens is carried out by the ministries of state organisation, media and intranet.

The Ministry of Digital Affairs enables digital participation in state proceedings by all those entitled to vote through the operation of intranet sites, directories and gaming applications. The administrators are directly elected.

7.1 Mediative[48]

Responsible for the mediative are the ministries of state organisation, media and digital affairs. Their task is to transfer information between citizens and politicians so that communication becomes possible through which the state can be jointly managed. The transmission of information takes place between citizens, citizens and politicians, and between politicians. For the transmission, the three responsible ministries provide the appropriate means and operate the facilities, offices and institutions of state law. Through the information, the work of government becomes comprehensible to the citizens and through the instructions of those entitled to vote, the work of government becomes controllable. The ministries of state organisation, media and digital affairs provide political education and participation for the citizens. Political education is provided through the means of political communication. By being involved, the citizens learn how policy works.

The Ministry of State Organisation, together with the Federal Moderator's Office, is responsible for moderating communication between ministries and citizens and for conducting quorums and voting. The Ministry of State Organisation takes over the moderation of projects in which several ministries are involved. Federal Moderators are directly elected.

The Ministry of Media Affairs, through the broadcasters of the state media, ensures information and interactive participation of those entitled to vote, controls in state organs and education for humanity. Citizens are informed by politicians through state television and involved in broadcasts through the People's Computer. The intendants of the broadcasting authorities are directly elected.

The Ministry of Digital Affairs, with its voting computers, intranet cafés, People's Computers, lines, intranet sites, directories and applications, is responsible for legally secure and democratically controlled communication between politically, economically and privately active users. Participation in committees is no longer bound to place and number of

48§113.1 Media democracy

persons due to digital presence. Citizens communicate with each other and with politicians via the People's Computer on the intranet.

7.1.1 Political means of communication

The policy means of communication ensure the right of access to information. It regulates that the information of any state activity is published by the ministries of digital and media. Citizens are granted full access to information. This is granted to them digitally through the state media and in real terms through the External Service of the Federal Moderator's Office. In addition, citizens' participation rights are also guaranteed. Citizens can make enquiries or introduce new publication obligations.

7.1.1.1 State television[49]

Government Television broadcasts all elections and legislative processes, i.e. from the legislature. Citizens can participate interactively via their People's Computer. Government Television films, broadcasts and stores the programmes of political parties and elections of persons, as well as legislative proposals before they are voted on. Politicians travel around the country in the People's Motor Vehicle[50] . The population gathers in a publicly accessible square next to the People's Motor Vehicle and in front of their televisions. Together, they formulate programmes, candidates, laws or legislative proposals. These events are broadcast in real time on local or national state television, i.e. Local Television[51] or Government Television. Those entitled to vote can participate interactively as television viewers. This means of communication is mainly used for committees. Government Television is also responsible for filming, broadcasting and storing for public access content that is put to the vote during an election week.

---

49 §113.2-6 Media democracy
50 Ministry of Media - 7.1.1 People's Motor Vehicle
51 Ministry of Media - 9 Local Television

The state television channels Party Television[52] and Youth Television[53] provide information from the executive, mediative and judiciary to those entitled to vote, adults and children. The programme is shaped by the work of citizens and politicians, who actively participate in the production of the programmes. In Party Television, the state organs themselves report on their work in informative and entertaining television formats. In Youth Television, the content from the other four broadcasters is translated in a way that is suitable for children. Special attention is paid to reporting on the ministries of family and education, because those entitled to vote are as young as ten years old.

The Surveillance Television and free non-state media provide controls and information from the legislation, mediative, executive and judiciary. Freelance reporters, accompanied by a monitoring team from the Surveillance Television, are allowed into state agencies without prior notice to document conditions there. Undercover investigations and recordings are also permitted. Responsible staff from the ministries of security, justice and labour accompany the reporters in the monitoring team for legal prosecution in case of violations.[54] Citizens are allowed to report to this broadcaster which questions they would like to see asked of which institution. The decision-making process for selecting questions must be broadcast in real time on Government Television. In addition, freelance journalists and media houses are allowed in all economic forms.

In Educational Television[55] all state-funded educational programmes are prepared in multimedia form and can be learned interactively in digital form.

---

52 Ministry of Media - 10 Party Television
53 Ministry of Media - 14 Youth Television
54 Ministry of Security - 7 Police, Ministry of Justice - 5.6.3 Public Prosecutor's Office, Ministry of Labor - 20 Company Auditing Agency
55 Ministry of Media - 13 Educational Television

7.1.1.2 Intranet[56]

The country has its own intranet for communication between the people and the state. There are surveys to participate in, voluntary proposals on how to do things better, forums, groups, statistics, service by linking to ministries and games in the virtual country. The intranet is the communication platform for citizens, politicians and state employees. All policy decisions are digitally mapped here. All users formulate policy programmes, proposals and decisions together here.[57] Through interactive PC games, state management is to be made possible and entertaining for the citizen.[58] Committees in particular are prepared by submitting and rating proposals for the initial vote on the intranet.

Citizens can use the intranet to trigger a new election for any politician and dismissal for any state employees. Once a deselection quorum is reached, the new election takes place. Once a dismissal quorum is reached, the employment contract with the state ends.

Voting on constitutional articles, laws and directly elected politicians is done via voting computers in the intranet café of a town hall and cannot be done on the People's Computer. Through mobile terminal devices, the intranet can be used by citizens. The Ministry of Digital Affairs takes care of the construction, distribution and operation of the up-to-date technology.

8 Political structure

The political structure of the dynamic media democracy consists of institutions and participants. Institutions are the ministries and parties. Participants are politicians, ministry staff and all citizens. When the term "citizen", "people" or "population" is used in this book, it always refers to domestic nationals. When the term "affected citizens" is used, it refers to domestic citizens who are affected by the policies of an organisation, municipality, nation, International Union or company. This could be, for example, all residents of a city or

56 §113,2,7,8 Media democracy
57 Ministry of Digital - 12 Directories
58 Ministry of Digital Affairs - 14 programmes

all domestic students. Citizens can also lend out their vote to delegates of a party or to a council. In that case, delegates are added as participants.

The political structures grow and shrink with the will of the people. Depending on which ministry is administered municipally, nationally or intentionally, directly, indirectly or representatively, or which decision is made with the participation of the entire population or only of affected citizens, more or fewer institutions and participants are involved.

8.1 Nationals[59]

Nationals have state powers in their hands. They provide and elect the state personnel and decide on the course of action of any policy in the country. All nationals together form the domestic people. All nationals living together locally in a group of at least 5000 persons form a municipality. Persons are granted domestic citizenship if they are fathered by two nationals. Children of whom only one parent is a national are granted the citizenship of their foreign parent until they reach the age of majority. They have to choose between domestic or foreign citizenship until they reach the age of majority. Until the age of majority, these children are entitled to voting rights for the ministries of education and family. From the age of majority, these persons must have decided on a citizenship.

8.1.1 People[60]

The domestic people determine the constitution and thus the basis for state policy in the country. In about 50 years, continental nationals are to form the continental people. In about 200 years, all persons are to form the people of humanity. This is ensured by the foreign ministries through the communitarisation of policy areas, ministries and states within the framework of an International Union.[61]

---

59 §47 People
60 §47 People
61 Ministry of Foreign Affairs - 5 Communitarisation

The people unite to protect their freedom and rights in their country and to preserve their independence and security. Through sustainable development on the part of the ministries, the natural foundations of life are permanently preserved. The common welfare, equal opportunities, internal cohesion and cultural diversity of the country are promoted by the ministries of labour, economy, innovation, integration and family. In cooperation with the people, the Ministry of Foreign Affairs works for a peaceful and just international order.[62]

The people, consisting of those entitled to vote, constitute the sovereign nation, insofar as national sovereignty is not limited by the constitution. At the national level, the people can confer rights on elected politicians. Through a subsidiarity vote, these rights can be transferred to the municipal or international level.[63] The principle applies that state tasks are carried out at the political level that is best able to do so.[64]

8.1.2 Affected citizens[65]

Affected citizens are at least 5,000 nationals who are nationally affected by a state, corporate or cultural policy or political circumstance. They can take collective political action by sending an initiative to responsible ministries, or by casting their vote for an initiative quorum.

8.1.3 Civil rights[66]

Human rights comprise the fundamental rights[67] to which every human is entitled and which he or she must abide by while inland. Certain fundamental rights, or parts thereof, are only available to nationals as soon as the rights concern state management. In addition, civil rights for nationals include

---

62 §49 Purpose: BV Art.2
63 §50 Nation: BV Art.3
64 §52 Subsidiarity BV Art.5a
65 §48 Citizens affected
66 §22 Freedom of movement, §23 Freedom of establishment: BV Art.24, §39 Civil rights: BV Art.37, §40 Acquisition and loss of civil rights: BV Art.38
67 §1-38 Fundamental rights

political rights and social rights.[68]

Nationals have international, national and municipal electoral and voting rights. The international electoral and voting right is limited to those international procedures in which the inland is involved. Municipalities may administer themselves and thus limit the number of those entitled to vote to those nationals of a municipality. Within cultural protection areas, persons with characteristics determined by municipal law may be excluded from the right of freedom of establishment or freedom of movement.

If voting is compulsory, nationals may be required to vote and face sentences for non-compliance. Manipulation of the opinion or voting of those entitled to vote is not permitted. No one may be excluded or treated differently, favoured or disadvantaged on the basis of voting behaviour, expression of political opinion or membership of party wings or constituencies.

The acquisition or loss of civil rights is linked to domestic nationals and is regulated by descent, marriage and adoption. The number of residence permits and naturalisations is determined by the people through a quota of foreigners. The Ministry of Integration is responsible for the laws and procedures.[69]

Foreigners can be naturalised. Naturalised persons have electoral and voting rights for statistical purposes. The evaluation continuously measures how far away foreigners would vote from nationals. If there are strong differences, the Ministry of Integration ensures further polls and eliminates parallel societies or terrorist aspirations.

8.2 Town Halls[70]

All ministries have at least one office in the town hall and take care of the implementation of the ministers' decisions. The ministries' offices are responsible for all citizens' questions on legislation and law implementation, depending on which

---

68 §39-42 Civil and political rights, §43-45 Social rights
69 Ministry of Integration - 4 Citizenship and Aliens Law, 7 Immigration
70 §41 Exercise of political rights: BV Art.39

ministry enacts or has enacted the law. Either the deputy minister occupies the office or the municipal minister, if the ministry is administered municipally. The ministries of economy are the exception. Town halls in the capital city of a Barter Economy Zone have an office for the elected deputy minister for Barter Economy. Town halls in a Social Village have one office for the elected deputy minister for Planned Economy. All other town halls have two offices for the deputy ministers of the ministries of Free Market Economy and Social Market Economy.

8.2.1 Intranet café[71]

The intranet café is the central contact point for citizens in every town hall when it comes to elections, voting and notarised work on the intranet. It is run by the Ministry of Digital Affairs.[72] Citizens can turn to the information desk in the intranet café with any concerns. Depending on which ministry is responsible, citizens are directed to the appropriate staff in the town hall. In case of waiting times, citizens receive a radio sensor that flashes when it is their turn. The intranet café serves as a waiting area. In the intranet café, there are computers on tables with admission to the intranet to participate in domestic political processes. At the information desk, citizens' People's Computers can be repaired or new People's Computers of various types can be purchased. People's Computers enable citizens to participate in the political processes anywhere inland. Current referendums and upcoming elections and votes are displayed on a large screen. It also shows on which dates and occasions a People's Motor Vehicle will come to this city.

---

71 §41 Exercise of political rights: BV Art.39
72 Ministry of Digital Affairs - 11.1 Intranet Café

8.2.1.1 Election week[73]

During election week, voting on politicians, laws and constitutional articles is held in the permanent voting booths in the Intranet Café. All those entitled to vote can cast their votes within one week, no matter which town hall in the country they are in. In large cities, the polling booths can also be mobile and placed in public places. The last voting day of the week is the non-working day of the week. In an International Union, the last day for all is the day on which the last member state had its non-working day of the week. Only when all citizens have had their non-working day of the week may the voting results be announced.

In order not to put too much strain on the citizens' willingness to vote, only 5 election weeks may be held within a 52-week period. Since the capacity to absorb political information varies among humans, a maximum number of votes must limit information overload and excessive demands on those entitled to vote. During an election week, the state media report on the contents of the ongoing voting. In order to limit the flood of information here as well, a maximum of 5 deciders may be voted on at the same time.

Only during the budget vote may an unlimited number of votes be held. It is possible to hold up to three consecutive voting weeks in which the many votes can be spread out.

8.2.1.2 Voting booths

In the intranet café, there are specially secured voting computers in voting booths where the voting is held. The voting booths are built like old fully glazed telephone booths. The telephone booth has frosted glass with lighting at the top, opaque panelling in the middle and clear glass at the bottom so that it can be seen from outside that there are only two feet in the voting booth. The voting computer is equipped with a touch screen, fingerprint scanner, iris scanner and printer for the voting receipt. The election receipt contains the personal details of the voter, namely the name and what was voted

---

73 §88 Election weeks

for. The voting record is sent to the People's Computer in the access directory because the personal data was retrieved for the verification of eligibility to vote. This allows for double-checking during recounts. The receipt is printed from a paper roll like the receipts in the supermarket. However, it cannot be torn off, but runs past a viewing window onto another role containing printed receipts. Through the viewing window, voters can check their name and voting result again. By opening the door of the voting booth, the role continues to rotate and the voting result is no longer visible through the viewing window. The container with both roles is locked, sealed and video-monitored. The roles are much larger than the roles for the till receipts from the supermarket. Only if recounts are required, the roll bins are opened to count the receipts of the corresponding election. If the bin is full, the full and empty roles are changed. The bin looks like an oversized audio cassette. Any movement and storage of the role with the receipts of past election results must be monitored seamlessly by video, as must the storage location.

Mobile voting booths store the voting results and only when the booths are back at their secured storage location is the data read out and sent via the secure extra line in the town hall to the data centre in the capital city of the Ministry of Digital Affairs. This process, too, must be seamlessly video-monitored. The Government Television transmits the images of all surveillance cameras in the split screen via an intranet channel.

8.3 Politician[74]

Party members contest the election of persons to become regional or national politicians. National political offices require a degree in the relevant field with a minor in political science. In the Ministry of State Organisation, political science is a major.

Regional politicians are citizen moderators, municipal judges or municipal delegates if the citizens use a municipal party council.

---

74 §59 Politicians

National politicians are the Federal Moderators, Ministers, Presidents of the Central Bank, intendants, administrators, judges and deputy ministers in the Council of Ministers if the ministry affected is administered nationally.

Transitions from regional politicians to national politicians and vice versa are possible. In doing so, the professional qualifications must be met. The required studies for the national political level are offered to regional politicians on a part-time basis. Registration for the final examination is possible at any time, even without studying. However, those who do not pass must first complete the degree programme.

8.3.1 Minister[75]

Ministers are the directly elected heads of ministries. They exercise leadership in their ministry according to their programme and the applicable laws and constitutional articles. They are able to make proposals for new laws and amend or abolish old laws and have the affected population negotiate and vote on them directly or in the annual budget vote. Norms below the law can be determined directly by ministers. Their legislative and law-making power is subject to citizen participation in the event of a participation, veto, repeal or deselection quorum. Ministers may be responsible for a municipality, a nation or for several nations. For which of these political levels a minister is to be elected is decided by the affected population in a subsidiarity vote. If not only ministers in a ministry have Law-making or judicial responsibilities, these senior officials must also be elected using the same election of persons process as ministers. The term of office of directly elected persons ends as soon as their deselection quorum has been met.

75§98 Ministers: BV Art.148

8.3.1.1 Working conditions for ministers

Ministers may resign at any time and then have a period of 3 months in which they still have to work after their termination. Otherwise, the people determine the appointment by election and the dismissal by quorum. Part-time work is possible, but then at least two ministers are responsible for the ministry and must be elected as a team.

Part-time ministers each have their own deselection quorum. If votes are cast incorrectly, the ministers make this clear publicly and transfer the vote to the minister who is actually responsible. If there are attempts to deceive, this is a criminal offence of election manipulation.

8.3.2 Deputy ministers[76]

Deputy ministers are directly elected in each municipality. Those entitled to vote are those nationals of the respective municipality in the sense of the election of persons process. Each deputy minister occupies an office in the town hall of his or her municipality. He represents the interests of the local population in negotiations with the national or international minister. In doing so, he can obtain exemptions or unifications. He also implements the national or international requirements from the ministry's capital city. In the case of a representative democracy, he is those entitled to vote in the Council of Ministers or the International Council.

8.4 Ministries[77]

In the dynamic media democracy, there are 18 ministries that execute the functions of the state. These are the ministries of labour, foreign affairs, education, family, finance, health, infrastructure, innovation, integration, digital, justice, media, security, state organisation, Barter Economy, Planned Economy, Social Market Economy and Free Market Economy. All ministries fulfil the tasks assigned to them by the

---

76 §98.2 Ministers
77 §135 Duties of ministries: BV Art.42, §46.3 State, §99.1-3 Ministries

constitution and the population. As soon as ministry employees make, speak or implement law, the affected population has the opportunity to trigger quorums in order to participate directly. Through this participation, citizens can manage and monitor the activities of the ministries.

Ministers are primarily responsible for the implementation of programmes in ministries. Ministries can be administered internationally, nationally or municipally, except for the ministries of security and justice, which cannot be administered municipally. The people decide on the division of responsibilities between the municipality, nation and International Union of each ministry in a subsidiarity vote.

The party of each ministry is primarily responsible for drawing up programmes and critical opposition through Counter-proposals for policy decisions. In order to be able to represent the government and opposition in the ministry, the party has any number of party wings. The party wings produce legislative initiatives, Counter-drafts, Counter-templates as well as candidates for political offices with direct election and their election programmes.

8.4.1 Capital city and outposts[78]

Each ministry has its own capital city. In this capital city are the party headquarters, ministry office buildings and the council building where the party, councils or ministry meet in public. Depending on the matter at hand, they meet separately or together. The field offices of the ministries are located in the town halls of all municipalities. Multiple authorities, organisations and companies of the ministries, such as police stations, courts, schools or hospitals, are located in the municipalities. The Ministry of Foreign Affairs maintains embassies and consulates as field offices in every nation and representations to every international organisation.

78§99.4 Ministries

8.4.2 Create a new ministry[79]

The people can create a new ministry or abolish an existing ministry. Both are possible through a corresponding initiative. If a minister does not want to take responsibility for the activities of an agency that is located in his ministry, he can offer the population three options. First, in cooperation with the Federal Moderator's Office, he can hand over responsibility to another ministry. Second, he can shift responsibility to the municipal or international level through a subsidiarity vote. Thirdly, he can suggest opening a new ministry and introduce an initiative to that effect.

Before a new ministry can begin its work, its tasks and responsibilities must first be fully described in constitutional articles and laws, and a minister must be elected. There should be no more than 20 ministries in the dynamic media democracy so that citizens can keep track of governance.

8.4.3 Internal heterarchy[80]

Internal heterarchy is part of the state's administrative procedural law, which the executive state organs must adhere to. The organisation of work in ministries and state enterprises is not hierarchical, but heterarchical. The citizens rule and the state employees execute, this relationship is hierarchical. The enforcement of the norms advocated by the majority of citizens is ensured by the politicians. For this purpose, politicians work together with the ministry's non-directly elected colleagues in a college.

All state employees know their work rules and instructions received from citizens or elected politicians and laws. When it comes to the implementation of this will of the people, superior relationships are no longer necessary. All colleagues should document their performance statistically, have it audited by the Company Auditing Agency and make suggestions for improvement as soon as possible.

The organisation of work runs through predefined areas

---

79 §99,5,6 Ministries
80 §112 Heterarchical organisational principle: BV Art.182

of responsibility in which the service instructions are implemented. The negotiation of these service instructions takes place whenever there are new laws or government decisions. To change existing service laws, employees use their right to propose and negotiate changes in the colleagues. All these negotiation procedures must be broadcast simultaneously and unabridged on the Party Television Beta channel[81] and published permanently on the intranet.

All state employees have their area of responsibility and clear service instructions. However, if leadership is needed in a group, the leader is elected by the group. Either a deselection quorum of 60% of the group must be reached, or the group leadership rotates among all group members at mutually determined intervals.

8.4.3.1 Heterarchical working conditions

Heterarchy means that superior relationships are structured democratically. The way of working is characterised by the fact that work areas are fulfilled independently by the employees. The aim is always to fulfil the working plan and the will of the voters. If several employees have to work together, group chairpersons are elected whenever necessary, who can enforce or prevent decisions in democratic negotiations and, if necessary, by veto. If more than half of the group members are dissatisfied with the leader, the deselection quorum is fulfilled and a new election takes place. It is possible to elect several leaders and give them different areas of responsibility in which they may decide on the rest of the group. If necessary for the fulfilment of tasks, supra-groups and sub-groups can also be formed. This system is similar in structure and procedures to political structures and processes, except that it takes place within the ministry. Ministers are leaders for all departments of the ministry, politicians are leaders for individual agencies and individual group leaders are directly elected by their group.

If it is necessary to improve task fulfilment, a scheduled rotation principle for group leadership can also be introduced.

81 Ministry of Media Affairs - 5.4 Beta channel

Each group member in turn must then take over the group leadership. All group members decide by a 90% majority after which period it is the next group member's turn.

Within the ministries, there are independent organisational divisions, most of which have elected politicians as their main leaders. The staff at all levels must pay attention to their autonomy in execution and can only co-determine their behaviour through the working plan.

Work is done by workers at the national and international levels in the ministry's buildings in the capital city or capitals. If a new federal state is established, the citizens decide which capital city will be the ministry's new national headquarters. The workers at the municipal level work in offices in the town hall. All employees may also work from home if this enables them to fulfil the state service and working plan required by law.

8.4.3.2 Working plan[82]

The heterarchical alliance is created by the working plan, which is to fulfil the requirements of the law. The working plan is created jointly by all employees of a ministry. If a new law comes into force that affects the ministry's way of working, the top level draws up a working plan and submits it to all lower levels as a proposal. The lower levels can submit counter-proposals. Once all the volunteers have submitted their proposals, all the ministry's employees decide on the working plan. Where expertise is required, all affected staff members who have the relevant expertise decide on it. All proposals and counter-proposals can be accepted or rejected. If no proposal or counter-proposal finds a majority of 65%, it must be negotiated in an internal committee. The event is broadcast on state television and held in the "Solution Finder" format[83] . Those entitled to vote are all employees. Those entitled to vote on a particular area of the working plan can also only be workers who are skilled and work there. Citizens

---

82§137.4-7 Interaction of ministry staff at several levels
83Ministry of Media Affairs - 7.2.3.5 Solution Finder (Legislation Committee)

have the opportunity to intervene in the negotiations through a veto quorum by conducting the negotiation in a committee and taking the final vote on the working plan.

Different working plans may apply in different nations or municipalities, provided that the requirements of the law are nevertheless met. Local adaptation to the will of the electorate or the factual circumstances is desirable in order to ensure the equivalent state service everywhere in the area of accountability of the political level.

Working plans are renewed on an ongoing basis. This happens whenever new laws are passed that affect the work area or new proposals for more effective work strategies are adopted. All employees are entitled to submit new proposals to the responsible subject area for the working plan in the ministry. Individual new proposals are dealt with in the same way as proposals made when the working plan was first drawn up.

The national or international ministers and their deputies in the municipalities are responsible for the fulfilment of the working plan. The Party Television films and broadcasts the working plan. The control of whether the working plan has been fulfilled in accordance with the law is carried out by the citizens, the Company Auditing Agency and the Surveillance Television. Whichever of the three authorised parties uncovers a violation must publish it immediately. Citizens can report breaches to the Company Auditing Agency or the Surveillance Television. The Company Auditing Agency reports breaches to citizens via the Surveillance Television. The Surveillance Television reports breaches to citizens. The repeal quorum can be used to change existing working plans in a committee.

8.4.3.3 Right of final decision for ministers

Since the minister is responsible before the people, he has the right to veto all proposed amendments, the So-called right of final decision. The minister decides for himself how much he wants to involve the nationals in the amendment process via the People's Computer or the party wings. Ministers have the right of final decision in any negotiation process for the implementation of new laws or changes to existing working procedures. This right of final decision allows elected ministers to overrule all other non-elected staff in the ministry. When ministers exercise the right of final decision, they must announce it on the same day in the Government Television daily news.

8.4.3.4 Co-determination rights for employees

State employees are very knowledgeable in their work area and therefore enjoy the right to make suggestions. Humans always come up with suggestions for improvement when they deal with things over a longer period of time. Due to the internal heterarchy, there is an internal reporting system for improvements. In all ministries, measures are voted on with the executives. Measures include all changes from performance to service delivery to internal communication or control.

Anyone who is directly responsible for a service and has an idea on how this service can be performed with less effort or better satisfaction of the citizens should directly contact the responsible executive.

Employees have the option of convening a committee through a veto quorum of 40% of the staff. In these internal solution finding committees, all staff from affected ministries are entitled to vote. The final vote can only be annulled by the right of last resort.

Where employees feel ignored and feel a hierarchy forcing them to carry out measures that are considered pointless, obstructive or harmful, they have the right to complain to the Federal Moderator and report the incident to the Company Auditing Agency or the Surveillance Television. The Minister may carry out an internal control. The Company Auditing Agency and the Surveillance Television jointly conduct an external control, which is broadcast simultaneously and uncut on the Surveillance Television's Beta channel[84] . If there is still no improvement, affected employees may turn to the free media and publish the facts.

---

84 Ministry of Media Affairs - 5.4 Beta channel

8.4.3.5 Book of amendments

If something is to be changed in the ministry in general, there is a So-called Book of Changes. The amendment book is a part of the ministry's intranet page in the State Directory, which can only be accessed by ministry staff. Everyone from the minister down to the lowest staff member in a ministry can write any proposal in here. The period is about 3 months. At the end of the period, leading politicians of the ministry have to write an amendment manuscript from all proposals in 3 months and publish it as text or video internally in the ministry. Now all ministry staff have 3 months to rate and comment on each amendment. After 3 months, poorly rated changes are improved or deleted altogether based on the suggestions for improvement in the comments. Improved changes are published again as text or video and rated and commented on by all ministry staff within 3 months. It is important that changes are implemented immediately if they have a majority among the staff and do not necessarily have to wait for 3 months.

8.4.4 State employees

The requirements for state employees are part of the Administrative Procedure Act and include salaries and bonuses in addition to the following requirements. State employees can be all domestic nationals of the country. Jobs in the state service are all posts in all ministries and their agencies. All state employees are responsible for sovereign tasks with which an ethos is connected that is committed to the local culture and the democratic people of the state. A state is supposed to be run by the nationals and not by foreigners. In the long-term perspective, this claim is relativised, as the legal boundaries of countries will dissolve into the United States of the Continents and later into the united states of the world. Exceptions remain possible in cultural protection areas.

8.4.4.1 Salaries and bonuses in the state service

Salaries are based on the performance of the work done. The Ministry of Labour develops the requirements for performance measurement and determines the performance of state employees with the help of the Company Auditing Agency.[85] Public service salaries can vary by 10% if employees perform their duties reliably, quickly and with dedication. Whether or not this is the case is entered into the appraisal system by the superiors after the annual appraisal interview. In the appraisal interview, the superiors should then negotiate their rating directly with the employee. Wherever possible, citizens as recipients of state services are also asked to give a rating.

8.5 Parties[86]

The Ministry of State Organisation regulates the existence of parties and their rights and obligations in the following Party Law. There is one party per ministry. Each party has a thematic focus that corresponds to the ministry's remit and is described in the basic programme. With its wings, the party represents the permanent opposition to the incumbent ministry and accompanies its work critically and constructively. The Ministry of State Organisation ensures through state law that parties are integrated into the political processes of the state as part of the political structure. The legality auditors of the Company Auditing Agency, in cooperation with the Guardians of the Constitution, check whether the parties adhere to the proper procedures in doing so.

Parties promote the formation of the population's opinion by discussing and combining policy issues and government work from different ways of thinking. This work is carried out in working groups and at party congresses and is made available to the population via the intranet, state television, other media and events. Parties solicit different opinions and solutions from the citizens, feed them into the appropriate

---

85 Ministry of Labour - 4.8.2 Bonus-malus system, 20 Company Auditing Agency
86 §56 Political parties: BV Art.137

party wings and bring them into working groups there. In the working groups, the majority opinion is identified and processed in such a way that it can be implemented by the government.

Parties participate in the formation of wills by mapping different decision-making options in party wings. In the party wings and their working groups, laws are discussed, new proposals are drafted and the minister can coordinate his decisions with the different party wings.

Each party has the possibility to send enquiries to the ministries in order to be informed about certain issues. For their substantive work, the parties can also access the state institutes to obtain expert opinions or to have drafts examined.

8.5.1 Financing

All parties receive the same amount of money allocated to them in the budget vote. In addition, parties are allowed to accept donations and advertise for a specific amount with a specific purpose. Donations may only be directed to the party and not to party wings. All donations shall be distributed equally by the party to all party wings. All donors must be published on state television and on the party's intranet site with their name, occupation and amount of money. Each party is given its own policy foundation in which its funds are administered. Party wings are allowed to use party donations to fund party headquarters, election advertising or consultancy services by expert scholars on policy issues.

8.5.2 Premises and equipment

All parties are allowed to use the state premises and are entitled to at least 20% of the usage time and equipment in the premises. The national party headquarters are located in the capital city of the ministry and may use the council buildings for their meetings and office activities. The same applies to the municipal party representations in the town halls and municipal institutions.

8.5.3 Basic programme

Each party has a basic programme and thus defines the goals and tasks of the ministry. This describes the professional orientation and the areas in which the associated ministry has influence. The responsibilities that must be dealt with in the basic programme are described in the constitution and the laws of the ministry. However, in the course of party work, amendments may be proposed to these requirements as well. The basic information is in each volume of this book for all 18 ministries.

8.5.4 Party wing

Within each party there are wings that represent different opinions and policy options. Within the wings, attitudes to voting, own draft laws and policy programmes for the ministries are elaborated. On the one hand, to offer them to the ministry and the people for implementation. On the other hand, to be prepared in case the deselection quorum of an elected state employee is met and a new programme and candidate has to be elected.

There are any number of wings in each of the 18 parties. New wings can form for one or more solutions and also disappear again. It is always about the most popular solution to a particular problem in one of the 18 remits. The number of wings and currents within the party become clear through several election programmes and candidates vying for the offices in a ministry. The best proposal is valid. Which proposal is the most popular is decided by the voters.

There is no wing compulsion. Each party member can decide anew for each individual policy initiative, such as laws or service instructions in ministries, which wing offers the most popular solution here.

8.5.4.1 Party wings in the election of persons process

Party wings draft programmes for the governance of their ministry and bring the draft programmes to the pre-election of persons.

Party wings nominate candidates for the offices of politicians for the run-off election of persons. All elected state employees are subject to the deselection quorum, which the party wings encourage citizens to vote for when misconduct is described. This creates motivation within a party to seek more popular solutions or to point out faults of the minister or ministry.

8.5.4.2 Party wings in the legislative process

Party wings accompany the government's decision-making and legislative procedures. To do this, they can gather arguments and facts in working groups, which they make available to the citizens. They can issue recommendations for action to citizens on how to revolt against unpopular policy decisions, organise demonstrations, petitions and initiatives. They can issue voting recommendations for the borrowed votes of citizens that are non-binding for delegates and binding for party wing leaders. They can speak directly to ruling politicians in their ministry at party congresses and introduce non-binding recommendations for action through motions.

Party wings can introduce counter-drafts to legislative proposals, support proposed decisions on upcoming votes with arguments and facts, have votes lent out to them by citizens through their leaders and members, and put forward programmes and candidates for the election of persons. Party wings always offer voters a choice of possible alternatives.

8.5.4.3 Slogans

The party wings can issue slogans for all votes. For this purpose, the party wings decide whether to vote in favour or against and issue a corresponding voting recommendation to those entitled to vote. State television publishes in the news all the slogans of all party wings that issue slogans. If a party wing leader has been lent out votes, a slogan must be issued by that party wing. In the course of this, the party wing leader must confess in which way he/she awards the borrowed votes.

8.5.4.4 One-day wing

One-day wings are called party wings that are intended to exist only for a short time in order to solve a problem in the short term, win majorities and be able to introduce it as a legislative initiative. Once the law has been imported or a measure has been successfully implemented, this wing disappears again. One-day wings can also offer an alternative to all those party members whose views are not represented in any wing.

8.5.5 Party membership[87]

Party members are politically interested citizens who wish to participate in shaping the opinion and will of the people. They can join a party or several parties and leave again at any time. It is not possible to leave a party as long as a party member holds an elected office. All nationals can become members of the education and family parties from the age of ten. Membership of the remaining parties is open to all nationals from the age of majority. Entrance and exit may not be influenced or hindered by any party. The decision is made solely by the citizen. Membership of any party is free of charge.

Party members can join one party wing. It is possible to join several party wings if solutions from different party wings are popular in different subject areas of the ministry. For example, in the education party, the higher education policy of one wing and the comprehensive school policy of another wing could be advocated. Employees of a ministry can be members of the ministry's party. Politicians must be members of the party while in office.

---

87 §57 Party members

8.5.6 Working groups

All the contents that a ministry encompasses are represented in the working groups. The contents are defined in the basic programme. The working groups are named analogously to the departments of a ministry and deal with how the content of the basic programme can be implemented in a department. These are new proposals for concepts or how an existing department of the ministry implements the basic programme. The working groups are the same in each party wing, but can also work together if the members of the working groups decide to do so.

Working groups are constantly working on position papers for programme items in upcoming election programmes. This work is intensified the closer the deselection quorum gets to being triggered.

Working groups can draft initiatives themselves and must supervise initiatives by citizens who are not party members. At least one party wing that is most likely to agree with the initiative must agree to do so.

Working groups shall issue statements in which they factually justify a favourable or unfavourable position by arguments that correspond to the attitude of their party wing. This position must be expressed on all ongoing legislative processes that affect the working group's area of accountability. Delegates party wing leaders must take this voting recommendation into account, delegated party members may take the voting recommendation into account.

8.5.7 Initiatives, petitions, demonstrations and delegates

Alternatives are sought and formulated for legislative processes and existing laws, and voting recommendations are issued to delegates.

Parties are obliged to support citizen-driven policy participation, such as initiatives, petitions and demonstrations. In all these forms, citizens are dependent on finding many citizens who have a similar opinion and support the project. Parties are particularly specialised in this, because in their working groups they take up opinions and formulate recommendations for action for politicians. Party congresses bundle the work of the working groups into proposals that can gain majority support, because the party members vote and thus give a picture of the mood, which can be read off in numbers. Election campaigns are connected with street campaigns in which citizens are specifically approached and asked for support. Parties should make all this experience available to citizens who have never or rarely carried out such campaigns before. It is helpful if a party wing that shares the opinion of the project takes on these tasks. If no party wing can be found for this, the entire party is obliged to support the actions in planning and implementation. This work is then shared by several party wings.

Delegates, on the other hand, are representatives of those entitled to vote who cast the votes lent out to them on behalf of the citizen who lent them out. Citizens who lend out their vote tend not to be motivated to participate in the policy process themselves. Parties offer these citizens the free service of lending out their vote to individual party members or party wing leaders. Parties are therefore obliged to provide extensive public information about their plans, attitudes and decisions. Citizens who have lent out their vote can thus check whether or not they have lent out their vote to the right party member or party wing.

8.5.8 Party congresses

Party congresses are held in the council building of the respective capital city. Party congresses last between 2 and 5 days. During a party congress, all members of that party throughout the country are entitled to vote. There is no delegate system. Party members do not have to travel, they can vote with their People's Computer from wherever they happen to be inland. Those present on the ground have to bring their own People's Computer. As long as the party congresses are taking place, the voting on motions is going on. A deadline is set for this negotiation. It lasts as long as the party congress. This makes it possible for working people to plan to devote more time to their party's policies on these days. For representative party work, as many party members as possible should participate in the negotiation process over 2 to 5 days.

8.5.8.1 Legislative party congress

At a legislative party congress, substantive decisions are made on how to influence current government work and how to handle past government work on the agenda. In addition, elections are also held for the leaders of the wings and for the president of the party.

At party congresses, the wings each meet in small groups and all wings together in one large group. In the wing groups, common opinions and wishes from all working groups are formulated. In the mediation groups, the members of the wing groups gather in mixed small groups to divide opinions and wishes into two categories. The first category is for opinions and wishes that can be agreed upon or combined. The second category is for opinions and wishes that are opposite or mutually exclusive. In the large group, all opinions and wishes are voted on. Then, in wing groups with descending order of majorities, opinions and wishes are transformed into recommendations for action. As far as possible, all compatible opinions and wishes are to be combined. At the end, the party congress votes on all the recommendations for action and thus ranks them. The party wings can issue these recommendations for action to the politicians and voters on a non-binding basis and impose them on the leaders of the party wings, who are also delegates, as a binding voting requirement.

8.5.8.2 Programme party congress

The programme congress is held by each party wing individually. It is part of the election of persons process in which all party wings prepare for the pre-election. The aim of a Programme Party Congress is for all wings to engage in their programme work and prepare their programmes for an upcoming election. The programme party congress consists of a kick-off party congresses, wing party congresses and a final party congresses, all of which take place within 4 weeks.

8.5.8.2.1 Kick-off party congress

Programmes cannot be worked out in 2 to 5 days. Therefore, there is a kick-off party congress with all party wings as soon as the deselection quorum of a politician has been met. All party wings now present their positions from the working groups to the party members. In the working groups of the parties, proposals on shortcomings in the laws are collected and solutions are sought. There is competition for the best of many solutions. Until now, the solution path was, for example, right or left, conservative or liberal. Such wings can also form in the new parties, but they do not have to. A substantive orientation can include several policy directions from right, left, conservative and liberal.

All party members now decide on positions they like. Now it is decided whether a party wing will die out or be newly founded. If a party wing cannot enthuse enough party members for its position, the probability of a majority in the population approving this programme is low. Party wings that have few party members and lose elections die out.

If no party wing has a position that is suitable for an effective programme for the ministry, a new position paper can be drawn up.

8.5.8.2.1.1 Board interview

At the kick-off party congress there is the executive interview. Here, the leaders of all party wings are asked by all party members which fault analysis they follow with the deselected politician.

8.5.8.2.1.2 Position papers

Position papers are prefabricated programme modules that have been elaborated by the working groups in their thematic area. The position paper of a party wing thus covers all thematic areas. Like a construction kit, there are several places in the text with options for different formulations. At least 1% of all party members must participate in the formulation in order for the programme to be admitted to the election.

8.5.8.2.1.3 Motions

Motions are a way for party members to change the position papers more than was previously possible through the selection of programme modules. Through motions, all party members contribute their formulations to the texts. Motions can propose amendments or improvements. Sometimes a motions can change an entire text or sometimes only passages of text, down to individual words.

8.5.8.2.2 Wing party congresses

Party wings are also allowed to hold their own party congresses after the kick-off party congress to work on their programme. At the wing party congresses, there is advocacy and counter-advocacy. Position papers and motions are not only presented and voted on, but also discussed. This is to make it clear who is for or against and why.

8.5.8.2.3 Final party congress

4 weeks after the deselection quorum has been met, the final party congress must take place, at which the programmes of each party wing are decided. The following week, the campaign for the pre-election begins.

8.5.8.3 Candidate party congress

The candidates' party congress is held by each party wing individually. It is part of the election of persons process in which all party wings prepare the run-off elections. The aim of the candidates' party congress is to find suitable candidates for the candidates' committee. All party members who wish to stand for election gather in the party's personnel groups. Each candidate must represent a programme. The candidate decides for himself whether he will continue the existing programme, present his own programme or represent a programme drawn up by his party wing. Candidates do not necessarily have to belong to a party wing. All candidates are placed on the list of candidates at the Candidates' Party Congress. At the Candidates' Party Congress, party wings may pre-select candidates to be put forward for the run-off election and participate in the candidate selection casting.

8.5.9 Ethics commission

All laws, measures or programmes involving ethical and moral decisions are discussed in the ethics commission. In the ethics commission, the party prepares moral decisions to be put to the people. Arguments for and against ethically questionable policies are collected and prepared throughout the country. In this way, citizens should be able to assess moral positions in arguments. The arguments will be sorted into pro and con and a gradation will be made to determine the strength of arguments. These determinations are negotiated and made during the ethics commission.

In party meetings, members look for topics they want to work on. Then it is decided whether each topic will be discussed together or all topics simultaneously in different groups. After it is clear which topics have majorities and whether they will be discussed separately in small groups or together in the large group, the flood of worries begins.

To move from the large group to the small groups, the following procedure is used. Both groups come together in a circle. Music is played and all group members form a polonaise.

Once the polonaise is up, the beginning looks for the end and closes the polonaise into a circle. As soon as both groups are ready, the music is turned down and a chain is formed that constantly passes each other. Now the music stops. Now the flood of worries begins.

8.5.9.1 Flood of worries

At the beginning of the flood of worries, two persons face each other. They have 3 minutes to exchange ideas. Then the chain continues to rotate like in speed dating. The same thing happens on the intranet. Every user is connected to another user in the chat every 3 minutes. The task is to agree on an argument to be added to the list of arguments in 3 minutes. The list of arguments is identical on the intranet and in the hall, because the party members in the hall also work with their People's Computers. Every word spoken is recorded and written down via a headset. All arguments are given numbers. Duplications are deleted. Behind the deletion is an algorithm that recognises similar arguments and proposes all similar arguments for reduction to one. There are two screens in the room for this. Each group can see all similar arguments on its screen and deselect similar arguments until there is only one argument left. As soon as the majority of 50% in the group has deselected an argument, it is deleted.

The flood of worries are doubts about how the ministry might deal with the issue. Anyone who has a concern reports to the room or via the intranet and voices it. Then the party members tick off all the concerns they share or are sceptical about for reasons to be named.

Once the process is complete, groups are created for the most popular 10 concerns. All persons line up in the hall at one of 10 points and go to a room with video conferencing facilities for a real-time broadcast on the intranet. Audience members can join the appropriate group on the intranet.

There are two subgroups in each of the 10 groups. In group 1 those who share the concern and in group 2 those who do not. As the persons in the room divide up, one sees on a screen the number of intranet users who are on the pro or con side.

Group 1 talks about the advantages. Group 2 talks about the disadvantages. Both groups should look for valid reasons why a concern is justified by an argument. In the first round, everyone talks to everyone in their group. The topic of conversation in group 1 is why the concern should be shared. Arguments for this should be sought and sorted according to strength. The topic of conversation in group 2 is why the concern is unfounded. Arguments against should be sought and sorted according to strength. The aim of these rounds in groups 1 and 2 is to determine the strength of the arguments. In the second round, everyone talks to everyone in the other group. The topic of conversation between the group member from group 1 and the group member from group 2 is whether a pro-argument is stronger than a con-argument. The arguments should be sorted according to each other. For example, if the pro and con arguments can be justified morally or technically, there are the categories "moral" and "technical". Matching arguments are juxtaposed. This way, many pro-arguments can oppose few con-arguments. The members of the pro-group have to rate the arguments of the contra-group on a scale from 1 to 6 and vice versa the contra-group does this with the arguments of the pro-group. Those willing to compromise can emerge from both groups. They form group 3 with the two group parts A and B. In A are the former members from group 1, in B those from group 2.

8.5.9.2 Discussion

After 10 rotations in the flood of worries, i.e. after 30 minutes, the two groups meet. The discussion begins. Arguments may only be used once to persuade, but may be used as often as desired in defence.

Group 2 starts and gives a counter-argument. Whoever from group 1 now knows a convincing argument against it reports. On his People's Computer, he enters the number of the argument he thinks is apt. The majority of all group members decides which arguments will be put forward in defence. When an argument is defeated is decided by the group defending. If the other group is not satisfied with it, a compromise must be found or the argument can only be put forward by a majority decision of the whole party.

This is followed by alternating pros and cons of the groups' arguments. The group that answers also has the floor for the next argument. During this exchange of blows, all party members can join a third group and leave their previous group. In the third group, compromises are negotiated. Anyone who has an idea of how a compromise could be generated goes into this group. The group sets up in two concentric circles. In the inner circle are former members of group 1, in the outer circle are former members of group 2. Each pair that could agree on a compromise writes it on the list of compromises. Similar compromises are sorted out in the same procedure as similar arguments.

8.5.9.3 Final vote

At the end of the ethics commission, all proposed solutions are accompanied by moral arguments for or against a proposal, and for some, compromise solutions are offered that either reject or endorse the proposal. There is a question on the ballot paper. It might read, "Should THIS or THAT or NOTHING be done?" Under the capitalised words are "+" and "-" boxes as choices. Those entitled to vote have 3 votes to choose + for agree or - for disagree for one word at a time. A field next to it says "Set majority threshold", the selection of which puts the vote into a majority quorum and by which a proposal for a majority threshold can be entered into a numerical field. Below the question, all pro and con arguments are listed in descending order of strength. Behind each argument there are "+" and "-" fields as a choice. Those entitled to vote have one vote per argument.

Through this process, a party can establish majority arguments that can be used to morally and technically validate or challenge government decisions.

This process is similar to a committee, but takes place in the parties. However, the people may also hold the process themselves as a committee.

8.6 Councils

Each ministry has a party council and a council of ministers. While the Council of Ministers exists only at the national and international levels, the Party Council exists at the municipal, national or international levels.

Citizens can choose between direct, indirect or representative democracy at any time. In representative democracy, councils are responsible for the election of persons and legislation. At the national level, the Council of Ministers is responsible; at the international level, the International Council; and in the case of municipal self-government, the municipal party council. In indirect democracy, the party council is entitled to vote for votes for which citizens have lent out their vote to it.

8.6.1 Parliamentary groups[88]

In councils, members of the same party wing can form a parliamentary group. Through parliamentary groups, members of a council can divide into further sub-groups to coordinate a common course of action. A parliamentary group alone is inadmissible so that cartelisation can be ruled out. There is no factional compulsion.

8.6.2 Council of Ministers[89]

The Council of Ministers can be used at the national and international level. For this purpose, it enlarges or reduces the number of participating municipalities. At the international level, however, the Council of Ministers is called the International Council.

Meetings take place in real terms in the capital city's council building, as well as digitally through participation of all members via videoconference. If several ministries are involved in a piece of legislation, stadiums can be used. The meetings are chaired by the minister.

Because each ministry has a council of ministers, there are 18

88§58 Parliamentary groups: BV Art.154
89§101 Council of Ministers, §79 Venues

councils of ministers. If ministries cooperate in an individual case, the councils of ministers of the affected ministries meet together. In that case, a Federal Moderator chairs the meeting. Whether or not the Council of Ministers is used is decided by the ministers independently or by the citizens in a participation quorum. The Council of Ministers always meets in public and all its meetings are broadcast on Government Television. Meetings of the Council of Ministers are held using the same procedural method as committees, except that Council of Ministers members replace those entitled to vote among citizens in the audience and viewers. For sessions in the legislative process and programme committee meetings, the show concept "Solution Finder" is used, and in the candidate committee meetings, candidates are selected for the election of persons.[90] The only difference is that voting also takes place immediately at the end of a council meeting. If citizens stipulate it in a participation quorum, voting can also be held directly or indirectly. In this case, the Council of Ministers only prepares the template for voting.

8.6.2.1 Members of the Council of Ministers

The members of the Council of Ministers are the deputy ministers. They are elected in elections of persons by a majority of those entitled to vote. Each municipality forms a constituency and each municipality has one seat. Each member has a deselection quorum, the triggering of which results in the new election of the affected member.
Outside the meetings of the Council of Ministers, the deputy ministers work in their offices in the town halls. Ministers occupy an office in the ministry building in the capital city.

90Ministry of Media Affairs - 7.2.3.5 Solution Finder (Legislation Committee), 7.2.3.2 Programme Committee, 7.2.3.3 Candidates' Committee

8.6.2.2 Permanent tasks of the Council of Ministers for the ministry

The Council of Ministers is the body in which ministers and their deputies in the municipalities coordinate the execution of the ministry's tasks with each other. The aim of this heterarchical meeting is to ensure that all municipalities are equally well supported by a ministry. The members of the Council of Ministers discuss where which form of care is most suitable or desirable. Services may vary and municipal laws may prescribe different procedures. In accordance with the heterarchy in practice, the elected politicians in the ministries work together with the workers in a direct democratic manner. The Council of Ministers is at all times the group in which ministers and staff coordinate their needs. The deputy ministers have the executive task of implementing central decisions and local adjustments in their municipality through their office in the town hall.

8.6.2.3 Giving voting rights to the Council of Ministers

Citizens can surrender their voting rights. If citizens prefer to give up their national or international voting rights for a ministry to a council, they can empower and also disempower the deputy ministers of their municipality by means of a participation quorum or a veto quorum. This possibility exists at the municipal level only if 90% of the citizens of the affected municipality have lent out their vote to a delegate of the municipal party council.

By surrendering the voting right, the procedures change to the mode of representative democracy. In the mode of representative democracy, the Council of Ministers also becomes responsible for the procedures of election of persons and legislation. The Council of Ministers is convened or recalled by request of the minister or by the citizens according to a veto quorum or a participation quorum.

Whether the mode of representative democracy is used is decided by those entitled to vote, either for individual cases in a veto quorum or until revoked in a participation quorum.

The minister can at any time let the Council of Ministers have a say in his legislative processes. The veto quorum allows the mode to be changed during an ongoing procedure. Once this procedure is completed, the mode that was last decided after a participation quorum applies again. A participation quorum can make a mode permanent until the participation quorum has been met again and a majority decides to change the mode permanently.

8.6.3 International Council[91]

The members in the international council are the deputy ministers of all the municipalities of the nations involved. The International Minister chairs the International Council when the ministry is on the middle ring of the International Union.[92] If the ministry is on the outer ring, the national ministers take turns to chair. All ministers of the member states get the chair in alphabetical order after 6 months. Once all ministries of several countries have international ministers, they form a new nation. The International Council then becomes the Council of Ministers again. As long as the member states cooperate in the outer ring and no international minister has been elected yet, all national ministers of the affected ministry participate in the international council. As soon as the international minister is elected, the national ministers resign. All other requirements are the same as those of the Council of Ministers. In the election of persons process, in representative democracy, the international council can co-determine the wording of the programme after the pre-election and elect the international minister in the run-off election. In representative democracy, the international council can co-determine the wording of international legislation and treaty negotiations and vote on them. A participation quorum also allows citizens to give responsibility for voting directly to citizens or indirectly to delegates.

91§102 International Council, §143 International Government
92Ministry of Foreign Affairs - 5.8 International Union

8.6.4 Party Council[93]

There is one party council per ministry. It consists of delegates who have been lent out votes by those entitled to vote. Its action is considered indirect because delegates indirectly make decisions for citizens. It is convened by the party before elections and voting when citizens have lent out their votes.
The Party Council meets digitally or in real life before elections and voting in a public Party Council meeting broadcast by Government Television. The real meeting takes place at the council building in the ministry's capital city. The digital attendance takes place on the party council's intranet site, where delegates are connected to the real meeting via chat or video conference. The leader of a party council is elected by the members of the party council and re-elected via a deselection quorum.
The Party Council enjoys special rights of information and may invite and question state service employees to its Party Council meetings for this purpose. Party Council meetings are held in public. Members shall justify their position and decision on elections and voting to their vote donors. The Party Council shall cast the borrowed votes by the first day of the election week and shall make public the voting behaviour of all its members, except for the personal votes of its members, for which, of course, the secrecy of the ballot shall apply.
Those entitled to vote who have lent out their vote may cast their vote themselves if the vote was not in their favour. The borrowed vote cast becomes invalid.

8.6.4.1 Municipal Party Council

The municipal party council includes all delegates who live in the affected municipality or belong to the party's own local group. The municipal party council has a special position because there is no council of ministers at the municipal level. The municipal party council replaces the council of ministers there. For the municipal party council to be responsible, at least 90% of those entitled to vote in the municipality must

---

93§100.4-9 Party Council, §79 Venues, §141.1b Municipal Government

have lent out their votes to municipal delegates.

In the municipal election of persons process, the programme party congress conducts the programme committee after the pre-election and the candidates' party congress conducts the candidates' committee. The municipal party council votes in the pre-election and the run-off election. Through this, the municipal party council elects the municipal programmes as well as the municipal politicians and the deputy ministers or else municipal ministers if the municipality administers itself. In the municipal legislative process, the Municipal Party Council takes over the negotiations with the municipal or deputy minister and votes on them together with the minister. It can introduce initiatives for municipal laws and counter-templates.

8.6.4.2 National Party Council

The national party council includes all delegates of a party who live in the country. The National Party Council may send representatives to committees or be consulted by ministers. Its members cast the borrowed votes for votes on elections of persons and legislation at the national level on the first day of voting and announce their voting decision.

8.6.4.3 International Party Council

Where a ministry has been communitarised in an International Union, all delegates from all participating countries are members of the International Party Council. Its members vote on international treaties, elections of persons and to finalise legislation.

8.6.4.4 Delegates[94]

All delegates are members of the Party Council. Delegates are party members who have been lent out votes by those entitled to vote. They bring these borrowed votes to votes and assemble

---

94§65,2 Instruction ban: BV Art.161, §57 Party members, §100,1,2,3

to debate voting decisions in the Party Council. Delegates can be ordinary party members or party wing leaders.

8.6.4.4.1 Party members

Those entitled to vote lend out their vote to a party member if they know that person and know that that person's opinion is closest to theirs. In this case, the selected party member is the delegate. Delegates should know those entitled to vote and talk to them as regularly as possible about their policy stance. Delegates are not bound by the voting behaviour of party wings when casting their votes, but award borrowed votes in the sense of those entitled to vote. They can make each voting decision differently for each individual case and only follow the requirements of their vote donors. Since persons may be members of more than one party, a person may be a delegate to a maximum of 3 parties. Delegates may represent a maximum of 100 those entitled to vote. Above this number, personal knowledge can no longer be guaranteed.
Delegates may vote in secret for themselves personally, but no secrecy applies to borrowed votes. Delegates are obliged to disclose their voting behaviour for borrowed votes to the person who lent out the vote to them. Such disclosure shall be communicated no later than the day before the commencement of the election week. Those entitled to vote shall agree with their delegates directly on how the notification is to be made. As members of the Party Council, their votes shall be published. Excluded from publication are the personal voting decisions of delegates and the personal details of those entitled to vote who have lent out their vote. Borrowers are given a number when they lend out their vote and can look up their number in the Party Council voting list and see what their vote was for.

8.6.4.4.2 Party wing leaders

Those entitled to vote lend out their vote to a party wing leader if they agree with the basic programme and the publicly announced position of the party wing. In this case, the party wing leader is the delegate who casts the borrowed vote in the voting. In contrast to the personal conversation and acquaintance bond between individual delegate party members, those entitled to vote do not care for direct contact with party wing leaders. Here, information is one-sided, with the party wing publishing its position from the working groups and party congresses, thereby signalling to those entitled to vote how they will decide in the coming vote. Party wing leaders who are delegates must abide by the requirements of their party wing and vote according to the instruction determined by a majority of the party wing members. Each party wing leader may represent an unlimited number of those entitled to vote. Party wings shall publish basic programmes in which they express their position. Voting behaviour shall be determined on a case-by-case basis by a majority of the members of each party wing and published by the wing leaders. For this purpose, digital polls are sent out via the People's Computers of all party wing members. They are not necessarily asked to indicate their own voting behaviour, but the one that they think best fits the basic programme of the party wing. Spokespersons for this unification of party members are called party wing leaders and are directly elected by the members of the wing they represent.

8.6.4.5 Lending out voting rights to the Party Council

Those entitled to vote can lend out their vote to a party member or party wing leaders and get it back. They can also distinguish whether and which of their votes for the municipal, national or international level they want to lend out. This option is available for all 18 ministries, for all votes on persons, laws and government decisions put to a vote.

Citizens who wish to lend out or retrieve their vote can do so at any time at the voting computer in the town hall. Lending out is valid either in the context of a voting for further voting in that individual case or generally for all voting for a ministry or ministries. To do this, either the name of a party member and their profile in the Persons Directory must be selected, or the name of a party wing.

Citizens who have lent out their vote can still participate in any election and voting. To do so, they can choose to vote differently from their delegate and cast their vote themselves. The vote of those entitled to vote shall always count first. Only if those entitled to vote have not cast a vote by the end of the voting period will the delegate's borrowed vote cast count. The voting computers automatically detect these double votes and always withdraw the delegates' borrowed voting right or cancel the corresponding borrowed vote cast by delegates. The delegates are not informed of who has cast their own vote, the secrecy of those entitled to vote applies.

Borrowed votes may only be used to replace votes that must be cast via the voting computer in the town hall. Opinions expressed in committees, ratings or comments made via the intranet and People's Computers are not affected. Citizens who have lent out their vote cannot be expected to follow all the committees to see if they should intervene because their delegate is not acting in their interests but is determining the ratings with all his lent out votes.

8.6.5 Scientific Advisory Board

Each party and ministry may establish a Scientific Advisory Board consisting of all necessary competent state employees. Its members must be temporarily released from other services to serve on the Scientific Advisory Board.

The members are scientists at a state school or college and are experts in a scientific field that is currently necessary in a legislative process. Children are explicitly included here. Such citizens can be appealed to the scientific advisory board. Whether they are appointed depends on the results from Company Auditing Agency tests and surveys or grades. They are invited to be panelists at ministry, party or committee meetings.

Each ministry and each party can obtain scientific assessors from the institutes and subject areas of the colleges in order to provide scientific justification for policy projects. At least three assessors should always come from different colleges. This prevents scientifically different views from leading to different forecasts for the policy project. If this happens nevertheless, at least 10 expert opinions from different colleges are requested and the assessors meet with the politicians for solution finding.[95]

9 Political processes

Political processes are understood to be all procedures that take place between political structures. The most important democratic procedures are quorums, committees, elections and voting. The procedural structure describes the sequence in which procedures are applied and by whom.

9.1 Dynamic democracy[96]

The dynamic media democracy is able to dynamically adapt the degree of its directness to the will of the people. For this purpose, the procedures for elections of persons, legislative processes and government decisions offer a direct, indirect or representative way.

In order to be able to introduce dynamic media democracy into existing representative democracies, the existing procedures are first adapted to the representative way. The normal state is indirect democracy with directly elected politicians in government. As a deviation from the normal state, citizens participate in the government by committee to take over direct management. The degree of this directness is again dynamic. In the weakest case, only voting is direct; negotiated procedures for templates can be indirect or representative. In the strongest case, a committee takes over the management of an entire ministry and the exchange of all personnel in the

95 Ministry of Media Affairs - 7.2.3.5 Solution Finder (Legislation Committee)
96 §46.5 State, §83 Flexible democracy

ministry, including politicians. Representative procedures are considered an exception when citizens are tired of voting. Voting fatigue is when there is less than 40% participation by those entitled to vote in an election or voting. Then a participation quorum is automatically triggered.

The dynamic arises in the individual case and at the responsible political level. Citizens and politicians can choose the direct, indirect or representative route for each individual case, with the citizens retaining the final decision-making right.

The motivated citizens make a long-term commitment to a political profession and party. The interested citizens use their knowledge from education and profession to contribute their expertise to decision-making in hearings, committees and discussions. They get involved when their profession or interest group is currently in the public spotlight and a law is to come that affects them. Disinterested citizens can do three things. First, lend out their vote to party members or party wing leaders. Second, they can only go to the town hall for voting during election week and not to the discussion forums on the intranet, interactive broadcasts on state television or the committees. Thirdly, they can cast their vote to the responsible council through the participation quorum if there are enough disinterested citizens.

With a successful government, citizens become tired of voting. They may then participate less and lend out or cast their vote. However, if the government creates reform bottlenecks and crises, citizens can participate more again or reclaim their borrowed or cast vote. In this way, citizens who complain about the state of the country can be asked to change it themselves.

The political processes of the dynamic media democracy are flexible. They adapt to the popular will for more or less say. Ministers are empowered to lead their ministry through the election of their programme and their person. During this leadership, there will be contentious issues. What is a contentious issue is decided by the ministers and citizens. If ministers have doubts or remorse about decisions, they may ask the people or the relevant council for help. If citizens hear from news reports about decisions made by ministers that they think are dubious, they can convene a committee through a veto quorum.

9.2 Political rights[97]

Political civil rights are special fundamental rights for nationals and naturalised foreigners. Binding to these are political rights that make it possible to freely form opinions and cast undistorted votes at all political levels.

Political voting rights are available to nationals from the age of 10 for the ministries of education and family, and from the age of 18 for all other ministries. Basically, political rights allow those entitled to vote to vote on laws and politicians under which they live.

The Ministry of State Organisation ensures political rights for citizens by having the Federal Moderator's Office match citizens with politicians. It ensures that citizens' interests meet the actual responsible politicians so that state service employees carry out citizens' interests. The exercise takes place in public squares, demonstrations, in studios of state television or People's Motor Vehicle[98] , the intranet cafés and voting booths of town halls and on the intranet. These real and digitally conducted political processes are committees, petitions, quorums, surveys, initiatives, elections and voting at the international, national and municipal levels.

Political rights ensure that nationals can participate in domestic governance. They can vote on laws that affect them. If they are affected by state employees with Law-making (legislative), executive (executive), judicial (judiciary) or mediating (mediative) functions, those entitled to vote can elect and vote out those politicians.

The simultaneous exercise of political rights in several nations or municipalities is inadmissible because those entitled to vote can then vote more than once, thereby undermining equality of voting rights. Prisoners are nationals who have caused damage to the state and its community and are suspected of

---

97§35 Political rights: BV Art.34, §41 Exercise of political rights: BV Art.39, §84 Political civil rights
98Ministry of Media - 7.1.1 People's Motor Vehicle

continuing to harm the community until they have served their sentence. The fundamental right to freedom and the exercise of political rights is only granted to a limited extent during an imprisonment.[99]

9.2.1 Free will formation

Free will means the freedom to obtain information from all sources and to express one's own opinion freely at any time, as long as this does not violate the fundamental rights of other citizens.

The ministries of state organisation, media and digital affairs support citizens in the free formation of will by creating and moderating communication opportunities. Censorship is only permitted if it deletes offences against third parties. The deletion must be approved by the victims or the content can remain with a note that it has been prosecuted and punished under criminal law.

The Ministry of State Organisation monitors the guarantee of a free formation of will and the undistorted casting of votes through the coordination of all responsible ministries as well as through voluntary citizens as election observers. The Ministry of Media Affairs is responsible for the media processing of political events to enable the free formation of opinion.

9.2.2 Unbiased voting

The ministries of state organisation, media and digital affairs ensure that the vote is undistorted. They ensure that citizens are given the opportunity to negotiate on projects in such a way that a text can be produced on which those entitled to vote can vote. Voting must be free, equal and secret. Freedom can only be restricted by a duty. Voting is compulsory in the case of constitutional amendments or in the case of vote rigging. The votes are to be counted equally, the So-called equality of votes must be fulfilled. The only exception is due to the number of those entitled to vote in a municipality

---

99Ministry of Justice - 7.5.1 Restriction of rights

electing deputy ministers. Accordingly, in representative democracy, more or fewer entitled to vote can be represented by deputy ministers if there are different numbers of domestic nationals living in municipalities and thus the constituencies are of different sizes. The difference must not be greater than 5,000 those entitled to vote. If, however, there are 5000 more those entitled to vote in one municipality than in another, the larger municipality is divided into municipalities. As soon as a municipality has reached 5000 those entitled to vote, it is considered a separate constituency. A municipality can therefore consist of several constituencies, in each of which a deputy minister is elected. The secrecy of the ballot may only be lifted for the prevention of electoral manipulation.

The Ministry of Digital Affairs enables uncorrupted voting through its own secured lines for the intranet cafés and voting computers, as well as its own secured wireless network of all People's Computers. For production, the Ministry of Digital Affairs has factories for hardware and software as well as sales and repair points in the intranet cafés of the town halls.[100]

9.3 Right to vote

The right to vote regulates who is involved and how in the procedures for quorums, elections of persons, committees and voting. Citizens enjoy the right to vote and may lend out or surrender it until revoked, except for committees and voting concerning the constitution. A quorum may call elections of persons, committees and votes. Through an election of persons, government personnel can be directly elected. Negotiations can be conducted through committees on programmes, personnel, constitutional articles, laws, regulations, investments, reforms or state service instructions. Through voting, all projects from quorums, elections of persons, committees and government decisions can be confirmed or rejected. Voting takes place in polling booths during election week. The veto quorum can be used to demand a recount of any voting.

Election advertising gives citizens, parties and ministries the

---

100 Ministry of Digital Affairs - 13 People's Innovation Company Intranet

opportunity to declare their intentions and win majorities among those entitled to vote.

The municipal, national or international right to vote is granted to those entitled to vote who are affected citizens. Depending on which level is responsible, the right to vote is limited to the affected population.

9.3.1 Recounts

If 50% of the voters doubt the result of the election via a veto quorum, the receipts remaining in the town hall are counted. All recounts are video-monitored, just like the constitutional referendums.

9.3.2 Election advertising

In election advertising, policies are presented by different party wings in a multimedia way. The ministries of media and digital support parties and ministries in advertising elections and voting.[101]

9.3.3 Mobile voting booth

In the dynamic media democracy, there is no postal voting. People who are not inland during election week cannot vote. Humans who cannot go to the town hall because they are physically unable to do so are visited by a mobile voting service. For this purpose, a mobile voting booth is brought to the voter. Mobile voting booths are always video-monitored from the outside, as in constitutional referendums.

---

101 Ministry of Digital Affairs - 2.1.2.1.2 Election Advertising, 15.5.6.3 Election Campaigns, Ministry of Media Affairs   - 5.3 Advertising

9.3.4 Electoral and voting right for nationals

The right to vote nationally is reserved for domestic citizens. Citizens aged 10 and over have the right to vote only for the Ministry of Education and Family Affairs. Citizens aged 18 and over enjoy full voting rights. All laws and politicians are elected by all nationals.

9.3.5 Electoral and voting rights for foreigners

Foreigners who have passed the naturalisation test and become naturalised persons are allowed to participate in elections and voting for testing purposes.[102] Naturalised persons have speaking rights on committees but no voting rights, not even through the People's Computers.

The data makes it clear what domestic foreigners would vote for. If there is a strong deviation, measures can be taken against the education of parallel societies. Testing purposes mean that naturalised persons are allowed to contribute their political ideas and opinions to the process, but their voting results are only displayed and not counted. Naturalised persons are not allowed to stand for election, but they are allowed to be members of one or more political parties. The background is that immigrant foreigners who do not wish to marry nationals and do not do so in subsequent generations should not enjoy full voting rights.

As soon as a new federal state comes into being, the foreigners who originated from the countries of the new federal state automatically become citizens of the new federal state together with the domestic nationals and are thus entitled to vote.[103]

---

102 Ministry of Integration - 4.2.3.1 Naturalisation Test, 4.2.3 Naturalised foreigners
103 Ministry of Foreign Affairs - 5 Communitarisation

9.4 Real and digital events[104]

Events where policy decisions are made are held in places that citizens can visit in real or digital form. It does not matter whether they are meetings of ministers with their ministry staff, council meetings, party congresses or committees. Real venues always have limited capacity, so unlimited numbers of citizens can only attend digitally via videoconference. The ministries of media and digital affairs are responsible for implementation. Real events take place in the state-political buildings of the capital cities. These are mainly old parliamentary buildings of the former regional and national parliaments. These spaces are shared by ministries, councils and political parties. Away from the capital cities, rooms of the former municipal parliaments in the town halls are used, but also large public spaces such as stadiums, market places or fairgrounds. Digital venues are the profile sites of the respective event. Here, video transmissions in real time and their recordings can be viewed.

As soon as ministers release the function, or citizens demand it by veto quorum, public state events also become interactive. Using the functions for contributions, comments and ratings, citizens can participate interactively in the event. Whether the participation is real or digital is irrelevant. The aim is to guarantee free admission for those entitled to vote at all times. Political events in dynamic media democracy are often convened by quorums. Results of these events are usually accepted or rejected by voting by those entitled to vote. This voting can only take place at the voting computers in the town halls during election week.

The political processes of the dynamic media democracy happen in the real and digital world. Devices provided by the ministries of state organisation, media and digital are always necessary for the implementation. People's own enterprises are run for the production of the devices and co-productions with domestic companies are carried out for certain devices.

Policy is framed as multimedia entertainment so that politicians and citizens can communicate with each other. The entertainment always takes place in locations that are mostly inland but sometimes around the world, for example when the

---

104 §79 Venues, §78 Publicity of meetings: BV Art.158

Ministry of Foreign Affairs is negotiating a trade agreement. Often, political processes are conducted in the form of tours, when several meetings are necessary. Several meetings deal with an issue in different or the same places until a result is reached that prompts the responsible ministry to take action. For example, a new law on road transport is negotiated by the Ministry of Infrastructure in three different major cities. The ministers make guest appearances at the local town hall and conduct the ministry's business from their ministry's office there.

9.4.1 Broadcast[105]

State television covers the policy events. Each meeting is organised with formats from the entertainment industry. These are for example stage shows, panel discussions, talk shows, news, interviews or video statements from the TV boxes[106] . The state television consists of different broadcasters that have different tasks of participation, information, control and education.[107] The Ministry of Media Affairs has equipment for events and for broadcasting the negotiations. The Ministry of Digital Affairs produces and maintains devices that present real-world events in the digital world and allow viewers to participate directly in the proceedings.[108] Events are prepared and followed up on the intranet. For this purpose, events have their own profile pages on the intranet with information videos, discussion forums and voting options.[109] The content of all events is stored in video, image, sound and text formats on the profile page for public access for 100 years.

---

105 §78 Publicity of meetings: BV Art.158
106 Ministry of Media Affairs - 5.7.3 Vox Pop Box
107 Ministry of Media Affairs - 5 State broadcasting
108 Ministry of Digital Affairs - 11.1 Intranet Café, 13.6 People's Computer
109 Ministry of Digital - 12 Directories, 14 Programmes

9.4.2 Participants

Ministers are there to implement the will of the voters. Councils are there to represent the electorate when the majority of the electorate has voted for them. Parties are there so that humans can find each other who have interest and knowledge in the same specialist department. Party wings are there so that people can find each other who share the same opinion and find compromises with humans who have a different opinion. In the real world, regulars' tables take place in inns and party conventions in stadiums. In the digital world, satellite images, simulation programmes and forums depict these events with their own pages on the intranet. For regulars' tables and party congresses, agendas are set in advance on the intranet and motions are submitted and discussed.

There is one party per ministry. Ministers are party members who agree to implement the will of the people in their specialist department. If a new ministry is needed or an old one has become unnecessary, this is negotiated and voted on in committee.

9.4.3 Devices

For the political processes of the dynamic media democracy, two devices are of utmost importance. These are the People's Computer on the one hand and the People's Motor Vehicle on the other.

The People's Computer[110] is a computer with binding to the intranet. It has a touch-sensitive screen, loudspeaker, camera and microphone so that the user can communicate with it. The People's Computer is the interface between the real world and the digital world, between one brain and many brains.

The People's Motor Vehicle is a truck with a glass container as a trailer. It has camera cranes and loudspeakers. In the course of time, other means of transport will take the place of the Truck. For example, the glass container could also float in on a zeppelin. No matter how the People's Motor Vehicle moves, it gathers the humans from the surrounding area via its

---

110Ministry of Digital Affairs - 13.6 People's Computers

loudspeakers with music and announcements to participate in an event. The People's Motor Vehicle is a mass communication tool with which communication events can be presented. Because humans can communicate best with each other when as many senses as possible are involved, citizens should meet for policy discussions in real life and not just digitally on the intranet.

9.5 Quorum[111]

You have to imagine the quorum like a barrel. Every vote fills the barrel. As soon as the barrel overflows, the quorum is triggered. When a barrel overflows is decided by the citizens themselves. The bigger the barrel, the more votes are needed to make it overflow. The limit at which the barrel overflows is the fixed majority of dissatisfied citizens.

In the dynamic media democracy, the quorum replaces the periodic election of representative democracy and acts as an instrument of control by the population over state action. Quorums have no time limit. As soon as a citizen is politically dissatisfied, he can assign this dissatisfaction to the appropriate quorum and express his dissatisfaction through his vote.

At the same time, it is a measurement tool so that politicians can gauge the dissatisfaction of their voters. When voting for a quorum, everyone is asked why. Politicians and parties thus receive valuable information. Politicians can respond to the criticism to discourage more those entitled to vote from adding their vote to the quorum for the same reason. Parties can see which programmes are well or poorly received by voters and at what time.

There are many different quorums that run permanently in parallel. They differ firstly according to what is to be newly elected, secondly according to how many votes trigger the quorum and thirdly according to which citizens are affected and thus entitled to vote.

---

111 §85 Quorum

9.5.1 Subject

A quorum always ensures that a certain political process has to be run-through. In the course of these processes, the prevailing conditions can be confirmed, changed or abolished. Humans, texts, numbers or possibilities of influence can be the subject of a quorum. Humans can lose their jobs by triggering a quorum, but are usually allowed to reapply in the coming electoral process. This means all ministers and certain elective posts in ministries.

Texts can lose their meaning by triggering a quorum. In the coming negotiation procedure, their meaning will be reviewed, confirmed, changed or revoked. This refers to all texts that have a policy-regulating effect on citizens.

9.5.2 Voting rights

All dissatisfied voters may submit their vote for a quorum at any time in the Town Hall or Quorum Directory. There is a voting booth in each town hall next to the intranet café, which is available at all times.

The vote for a quorum can only be cast once until that quorum is triggered. Once a vote has been cast in a quorum, it cannot be reversed. The point here is to punish unpopular phases in political action and activity. Once enough citizens have cast their vote in the quorum, it is triggered. The triggering can result in a measure or a voting. After triggering, the count is set to zero, all votes cast are erased and can be newly cast. After the death of a voter, their vote disappears from the quorum.

Not every citizen can always be entitled to vote for every quorum. Depending on whether a decision is at the municipal, national or international political level, only citizens living there or affected by it are entitled to vote. Every decision can be linked to a quorum. Therefore, decisions by state-owned enterprises, municipalities, the nation or international organisations can be linked to a quorum. In exceptional cases, affectedness can also be guaranteed beyond the political levels, for example in the case of consumers of a certain product. The quorums for which a citizen is entitled to vote are displayed in the Quorum Directory.

9.5.3 Term of office and period of validity

In the policy system of dynamic media democracy, the quorum replaces the periodic election. Once the set level of dissatisfaction is full, a corresponding measure or voting is held. Crucially, the quorum is open as long as a requirement applies, a politician is in office or a state employee is in service. The quorum would remain open forever or for life for very successful laws or politicians and judges. State requirements last indefinitely until enough those entitled to vote want to reform or abolish them. Politicians are only deselected when they have lost favour with the electorate. Periodic elections have the disadvantage that decisions are made for the duration of the election period. Politicians who are elected periodically can make policies that are harmful in the long run but favourable in the short and medium term.

Quorums are used to promote policies that ensure the long-term survival of humanity and the people and enable a rising standard of living. The aim should be that politicians think and act in the long term and not only until the end of a term in office. This makes it easier for politicians to make long-term decisions. According to game theory, if the end of their term remains open, it is irrationally defective to play. It is known from economic game theory that before the last move in the game, people like to play defectively instead of cooperatively because there is no longer any possibility of sanctions. This is not the case in infinite games because it is uncertain when the end will be reached.

9.5.4 Quorum Directory

Every decision that is linked to a quorum is given a profile in the Quorum Directory. This profile is the automatic redirect you get when you press the "deselection", "veto" or "override" button on the ballot paper during a vote. Outside of voting, citizens can fill out a search form describing their dissatisfaction. An algorithm then displays the various responsible politicians and laws that are responsible for the dissatisfaction. All current quorums are now listed and the citizen can decide which human or text would have to change to eliminate their dissatisfaction.

Once a citizen has selected the appropriate quorum profile, he or she presses the "Fill in" button. The citizen is now asked about the reasons for his or her dissatisfaction and how this dissatisfaction could be eliminated. An algorithm recognises similar concerns and suggests them. The citizen can now agree to these concerns via the "follow" button. Multiple choices are possible. Supporters and opponents of one or more quorums can form groups.

All details are published on the quorum profile page, but can be made anonymous if the citizen wishes. Only the postcode must be given.

Quorum Directory profiles dealing with the deselection of a politician are always connected to the politician's profile in the Labour Directory.

9.5.5 Coordination process on the intranet

The Quorum Directory gives users an overview with all possible links to the other directories. Each elected state employee has a field on their profile in the Labour Directory[112] showing the current percentage of affected citizens who voted for "deselection". Similarly, each law has a field on its profile in the Law Directory showing the current percentage of affected citizens who voted for 'repeal'.[113]

If users place a tick behind the percentage, the input mask for the deselection quorum opens. Here you can select keywords where the state employees have made faults and you can enter or upload texts, pictures or videos. For each quorum, the percentage is given with 7 decimal places, so that each individual can see how their vote affects the percentage. Everyone who has cast their vote receives a confirmation in their Access Directory, where their name, birthday and place

---

112Ministry of Labour - 13 Labour Directory
113Ministry of Justice - 4.7 Law Directory

of birth are shown alongside the percentage with 7 decimal places. Entries can be made via the People's Computer or by visiting a polling booth. The voting computer then issues a receipt showing the same information as in the confirmation in the Access Directory. This means that everyone who has cast a vote has a unique numeral that cannot appear twice. Similarly, any single change in the percentage of the quorum can be attributed to a single those entitled to vote. If there are irregularities in either of the two control methods, those entitled to vote must fill in on the ballot paper at the coming election or vote whether they had cast their vote for the corresponding quorum.

9.5.6 Opposition work of the party wings as a motor for a quorum

A quorum can influence all government work. The opposition plays the role of highlighting dissatisfaction and formulating proposals for improvement. This opposition work can be done by citizens, parties or deputy ministers. Any citizen can open a quorum in the Quorum Directory, if this has not already been done automatically. Once a politician of a certain party wing is in office, other party wings and their supporters in the population can voice their criticism and build majorities through a quorum. Party wings in particular advertise to affected citizens to participate in a quorum. Party wings inform the population about critical views of a policy proposal and inspire politicians to adopt different policies, especially when a quorum is growing in popularity.

The other wings of the party that are not in government or office also have the opportunity to address the minister with their concerns or to introduce Counter-drafts and Counter-templates. But if he disregards them, the opposition starts mobilising votes in the electorate for an appropriate quorum. The Party Television is obliged to produce and broadcast promotional videos for the deselection, several times a day for a week. In the production, the spokespersons of the party wing are the final editors.[114]

---

114 Ministry of Media Affairs - 5.3 Advertising

9.5.7 Majority quorum

The majority quorum allows all applicable majority ratios of votes to be negotiated in a committee and voted on by affected citizens or the people. For the first of these votes, the majority ratio of 65% applies. All other majority ratios are determined by the citizens.

9.5.8 Quorum limits quorum

What majority is needed to trigger a quorum is of crucial importance for the political processes. The percentage of affected citizens that triggers a quorum is negotiated in a committee. The following upper and lower limits apply. The lower limit is 10% and is reached in the case of decisions with a risk of discrimination that may severely burden a minority. The upper limit is 90% and is reached in the case of decisions with an absolute necessity of general compatibility that must be borne by many citizens for a long time.
As soon as 30% of those entitled to vote in a quorum consider its trigger limit to be inappropriate and press the "Adjust % limit" button on a quorum's profile page, the limit is renegotiated in a committee. In the voting that follows, citizens can enter a percentage. After the voting, all votes are listed in ascending order and the median, i.e. the middle of all percentages, emerges as the winner of the voting.
The citizens themselves are the most aware of how willing they are to deal with a politician or a law that they are not familiar with. Here, only knowledgeable citizens recognise the grievance and have a hard time mobilising majorities in the population to trigger the quorum. Therefore, the quorum should already be triggered in the case of a dissatisfied minority of, for example, 30%. In order to be able to decide more precisely, surveys should clarify how high the professional qualification of the population is and whether increased media education could lead to more participation.
In other areas, a minority may feel strongly disadvantaged and thus oppressed by the majority, which can increase the dissatisfaction of the individual to the point of radicalism. If

such situations occur, it is important to check where the votes are coming from. If they are locally close, a cultural protection area could be established there or the municipality could gain responsibility through a subsidiarity vote. If all this does nothing to alleviate dissatisfaction or provide an alternative, the majority threshold can be moved. In the responsible committee and the subsequent voting, however, the minority is dependent on the goodness of the majority, even if only 50% of the affected citizens.

9.5.9 Quorum quorum

Quorum quorum is a quorum for quorums, the triggering of which results in the establishment or removal of a quorum for a person or decision. 20% of those entitled to vote trigger the quorum quorum. Whether a quorum is needed, and for whom or what, is negotiated in a committee.

9.5.10 Deselection quorum

A deselection quorum is a quorum for politicians, the triggering of which results in new elections of persons for that office. Politicians and state employees have term of office for life until sufficient voters have voted for their deselection. Politicians may, of course, resign or retire at any time with 3 months' notice.

Every voter can deselect every elected politician once. As soon as the number of votes in the deselection quorum that once led to the politician's election is reached, the post is re-elected. The politician may stand for election again if he or she has not made any punishable deciders.[115] After a new election, the deselection quorum always counts as 0%. The election period therefore lasts exactly as long as the majority of citizens approve of the politician's behaviour. This can be one day or for life.

---

115 Ministry of Justice - 8.14.2.1 Public liability

9.5.11 Participation quorum[116]

A participation quorum is a quorum for the directness of democracy, the triggering of which results in the change of government procedure. Through the participation quorum, those entitled to vote can decide whether elections of persons, legislation and government decisions are made directly by citizens, indirectly by the minister or representatively by the council. These decisions are made by the citizens themselves either through the representative, indirect or direct participation quorum or through their failure to participate in voting, negotiations or elections of persons.

75% of those entitled to vote trigger the representative participation quorum. From then on, the procedures of representative democracy are applied and all those entitled to vote hand over their vote to a council.

50% of those entitled to vote trigger the indirect participation quorum. From then on, the procedures of indirect democracy are applied and all those entitled to vote hand over their vote to a minister or lend it out to a delegate.

30% of those entitled to vote trigger the direct participation quorum. From then on, the procedures of direct democracy are applied and all those entitled to vote cast their votes themselves in committees and ballots.

If participation in negotiations or voting falls below a certain percentage of those entitled to vote, a committee is convened by the Minister of State Organisation. Citizens are asked why participation is so low and whether they prefer a representative process for negotiation and voting by a council in one or more ministries. The committee may make voting compulsory for this voting.

The voting participation quorum is triggered as soon as less than 40% of those entitled to vote cast their vote. Excluded from this are borrowed votes. For all national votes, the Council of Ministers then votes instead of the citizens. In the case of municipal self-government, the municipal party council votes on behalf of all those entitled to vote who have lent out their vote.

The negotiation participation quorum is triggered as soon

116 §46.5 State, §104.4 Government decisions

as less than 1% of those entitled to vote participate in real or digital negotiations. Negotiations are then conducted indirectly by the Minister with his Ministry or representatively by the Minister and the Council.

The quorum for participation in the election of persons is triggered as soon as less than 20% of those entitled to vote cast their vote in the run-off election. Excluded from this are borrowed votes. Non-voters are asked to lend out their vote to a party member or wing. The committee may determine whether to hold a voting on a chain of legitimacy with compulsory voting.

9.5.12 Staff quorum[117]

A staff quorum is a quorum for government personnel positions, the triggering of which results in a committee. Which post in a ministry should be elective is decided by the population in a committee. If the office of a senior executive is directly elected, this quorum can ensure that there is no longer a direct election of persons, but that the ministry's personnel department is responsible for the appointment. In this case, 50% of those entitled to vote must be in favour.

If the office of a senior officer is filled by the staff department, the staff quorum can ensure that a direct election of persons is introduced. In this case, 30% of those entitled to vote must be in favour. The staff quorum is created for each senior staff member of a ministry on their profile in the Labour Directory and the Quorum Directory.

9.5.13 Initiative quorum

An initiative quorum is a quorum for proposals from citizens. As soon as 10% of those entitled to vote have cast their vote in favour of the initiative quorum, a committee is convened in the case of a draft or a vote is scheduled directly in the case of a template. The ministries and parties are automatically notified and must take a stand in the Government Television news.

---

117 §60,2-5 Eligibility

If the initiative is a draft, the responsible ministry shall convene a committee. The committee may be convened after 7 days at the earliest, so that counter-proposals can be submitted. The committee must be convened after 2 weeks at the latest. If several ministries are affected, the Ministry of State Organisation convenes the committee and Federal Moderators take the chair. If a template is submitted after the committee, it is put to a vote.

If the initiative is a template, the responsible ministry shall schedule a voting. The voting may take place in 7 days at the earliest. If a counter-proposal is submitted as a template within this period, it will also be put to a vote. However, if the counter-proposal is introduced as a draft, the deadline must be postponed by 2 weeks. The draft is then first worked out in a committee on the template.

In the voting, at least 60% of the votes must be cast in favour of the template. Responsible ministers are obliged to import the norms or implement the decision.

9.5.14 Veto quorum[118]

A veto quorum is a quorum whose triggering transfers a policy procedure to a committee. The veto quorum is only valid as long as the procedure lasts. It is used to intervene in ongoing procedures and to select the mode of direct democracy for the procedure in this individual case and to convene a committee. Controversial laws can thus be identified at the very beginning of a legislative process by citizens adding their vote to the veto quorum. If citizens or the party notice during the reporting of the proposed legislation that it would cause dissatisfaction among them or their clientele, they encourage those entitled to vote to participate in the veto quorum so that the legislative process continues in a committee.

State television reports on all new bills that the ministries or parties are working on and on all discussions in the Legislative Directory in which at least 30% of the users participate. In the policy debates, it becomes clear which legislative projects are so controversial that they would generate rising discontent in

118§77,1,3 Revision of the laws

the long term.

As soon as a bill is introduced by ministers or citizens, it appears in the Government Television news and in the Legislative Directory[119] . Citizens can cast their vote for approval, disapproval or objection on the profile of the bill in the Legislative Directory. Silence is considered as approval. Citizens can use "Dislike" and "Appeal" to lodge a veto.

Once the veto quorum of 30% of all affected citizens is reached, the law must be drafted and voted on in a committee. Once a law has been approved by voting, it is transferred from the Legislative Directory to the Law Directory and can only be amended or repealed by a repeal quorum.

Every year for the budget vote[120] all laws of the past year are listed. Behind each new law of the past year that has not yet been voted on, a cross can be placed at "approval", "rejection" or "objection". Silence also counts as approval here. All non-voters and all approvals are counted together but published individually. Here, too, the votes for rejection and objection count towards the veto quorum. The veto quorum ends after the budget vote. Either the quorum was triggered and the law is rewritten in committee or abolished. Or the law found a majority and enters into force the following day. After that, the law can only be amended or abolished by a repeal quorum.

9.5.15 Repeal quorum[121]

A repeal quorum is a quorum whose triggering results in a committee deciding whether a norm should be abolished or changed. The repeal quorum applies to all norms in the Law Directory, no matter how old they are.[122] This also applies to treaties under international law. If a law is already valid but its effect does not serve the desired purpose, a committee is convened on the valid law. The committee then decides whether the law should be abolished, amended or confirmed. State television reports on all laws passed in the past year and

---

119 Ministry of Justice - 4.7 Law Directory
120 Ministry of Finance - 9.5 Budget vote
121 §77,2,3 Revision of the laws
122 Ministry of Justice - 4.7 Law Directory

on all discussions in the Law Directory in which at least 30% of the users participate. In the policy debates, it becomes clear which laws are so controversial that they miss their mark in the long run. The repeal quorum is triggered as soon as 50% of those entitled to vote cast their vote in favour.

9.5.16 Revision quorum[123]

A revision quorum is a quorum whose triggering results in a constitutional amendment of one or more articles. In a constitutional committee, the article or articles affected are negotiated and voted on by the people.

The special feature of the revision quorum is that it is simultaneously an initiative quorum for constitutional initiatives and a repeal quorum for constitutional articles. Anyone who submits a constitutional initiative automatically opens a revision quorum. Anyone who casts a vote in the Law Directory for the amendment or repeal of an article of the Constitution thereby opens a revision quorum for that article. While authors of a constitutional initiative have already formulated the proposal for improvement, a constitutional committee still has to do so once the revision quorum from the Law Directory has been fulfilled. In this case, all the statements left by supporters of the revision quorum in their voting are brought to the constitutional committee as suggestions.

If the revision quorum requires the amendment of an existing article or the insertion of a new article, 2% of those entitled to vote are required to fulfil the quorum. If several substantively related articles are to be amended or newly inserted, 10% of those entitled to vote are required. If the entire constitution is to be amended or an initiative on a new constitution is to be introduced, 25% of those entitled to vote must meet the revision quorum.

The fulfilment of a revision quorum based on a suggestion or draft shall result in the convening of a constitutional committee. The fulfilment of a revision quorum, which is based on a template, results in a constitutional referendum.

---

123 §256 Revision quorum

9.5.17 Empowerment quorum

An empowerment quorum is a quorum whose triggering results in popular empowerment. All or part of the staff of one or more ministries is replaced and ongoing legislative processes are stopped. New elections are held and until the new staff is appointed, the Ministry of State Organisation or disaster management is responsible for the management of the ministry on a deputy basis.
Once 60% of those entitled to vote have cast their vote for the empowerment quorum, it is triggered. It can also be triggered by an approval vote if 60% of those entitled to vote do not approve the entire ministry.

9.5.18 Dismissal quorum

The dismissal quorum results in the termination of the affected state employees with three months' notice. The position is re-advertised, but the state employees dismissed by a quorum may not newly apply for the same position.
The number of those entitled to vote who are nationals depends on the area of operation of the state employees. Once 65% of the affected citizens have cast their vote for the dismissal quorum, the state employee is terminated.
In the Work Directory[124] , all state employees can be terminated by pressing the "Dismiss" button on their profile page. For example, 65% of all nationals want a new security minister or 65% of all parents of a primary school class want a new class teacher. In addition to the "Dismiss" button, there is also a button for "Rate". Behind it is the bonus-malus system.[125] State employees are rated by the citizens on how they perform. In contrast to the deselection quorum, votes can also be cast for the person. Increasing satisfaction brings the state employees a bonus, decreasing satisfaction lowers the bonus. State employees are dismissed if legal violations are reported or if the dismissal quorum is triggered.
If corruption occurs more frequently in a position, this post

---

124 Ministry of Digital Affairs - 5 Digital Administration
125 Ministry of Labour - 4.8.2 Bonus-malus system

can be taken over by a directly elected politician, because then there are more possibilities for control.

9.5.19 Subsidiarity quorum

A subsidiarity quorum is a quorum whose triggering results in a subsidiarity vote. It is triggered as soon as 30% of those entitled to vote are in favour of a municipal, national or international responsibility. This means that in order to make a decision at the municipal level, 30% of those entitled to vote in the municipality are required. At the national level it is 30% of the people and at the international level 30% of those entitled to vote in all the peoples involved.

9.6 Committee[126]

The aim of a committee is to involve citizens in the decision-making process of the ministries. Participation takes place only when citizens request it by quorum or when ministers request it on their own initiative or when the constitution prescribes the committee procedure. Participation takes place through the media of television and intranet, allowing all affected citizens to participate virtually in the real public event. Participation involves the formulation of texts for state measures, such as laws, regulations and election programmes, the selection of executives and the democratic voting on them. Decision-making primarily concerns all Law-making decisions, such as laws. It also concerns the election of politicians, such as ministers and senior ministry officials. A committee can also negotiate and schedule a voting on the pardon of a prisoner. Committees involve politicians, academics, affected persons, party wing leaders and citizens who are responsible for or interested in the subject area concerned. Experts designated by the committee may be called in for advice.
A committee has achieved its objective when, after a final vote by affected citizens, a state measure is enacted, modified or abolished.

126§92 Committees: BV Art.157

9.6.1 Purpose

The committee is the central instrument of political processes in the dynamic media democracy. Citizens are involved in the policy process through committees. Councils and ministries also use committee procedures in their negotiations. Committees give decision-makers and their affected parties the opportunity to negotiate and vote together on measures according to a predefined procedure. Accordingly, both groups of people, i.e. decision-makers and those affected, can force the other group to work together in a committee. Which participants are involved as experts is determined by the person who convenes the committee. Between the convening and the start of the meeting, other persons can be invited as experts. It is crucial that deciders and affected persons alike can nominate and invite experts.

9.6.2 Procedure

Which procedure is used on the respective committee depends on the concern. The standard procedure is the show format "Solution Finder[127] ". However, other procedures from the ministries for media[128] and digital[129] are also possible. The committee procedure adapts to the decision to be taken. Whether it is the election of persons, decisions on legislative texts or other government decisions that the state issues for employees or citizens, the committee procedure can be used for every issue.

At the event, solutions and ways are found to formulate programmes, laws or treaties in such a way that they can be passed by a majority. Whether the majority is then achieved is shown in the voting on the voting computer in the town hall during the election week.

---

127 Ministry of Media Affairs - 7.2.3.5 Solution Finder (Legislation Committee)
128 Ministry of Media Affairs - 7.2.3 Shows, 11.1.1.3 People's Control, 12.3.4 Shows
129 Ministry of Digital Affairs - 14 programmes

9.6.2.1 Committees in the legislative process[130]

A committee can be convened before, during or after a legislative process. It is a central part of direct legislation. Ministers can choose this route at any time, councils need a majority of 65% and citizens must meet the necessary votes in a veto quorum or repeal quorum. Committees fulfil the task in the legislative process of formulating the text of the law in such a way that the majority of those entitled to vote can agree to it. The show format "Solution Finder" is used as the procedure.[131] The procedure remains the same whether it is used to describe projects to be used at the municipal, national or international level or for party work.

9.6.2.2 Committees in the election of persons process[132]

In the election of persons, committees are held whose procedures differ from those of the legislative committees. Since the election of persons process is divided into two sections by the pre-election and the run-off election, two committees are also held. First, in the programme committee, successful election programmes from the pre-election are transformed into up to three programmes for the run-off election. Second, the candidates' committee tests candidates who wish to implement the programme in order to field two candidates per programme for the run-off election.

9.6.2.3 Mandatory committees[133]

Committees must be convened when politicians and their programmes are selected, when the constitution is amended or when international law treaties are negotiated. In the case of criminal misconduct or disregard for the will of the people by politicians, a committee of enquiry is held.

---

130 §96 Committees in the legislative process
131 Ministry of Media Affairs - 7.2.3.5 Solution Finder (Legislation Committee)
132 §95 Committees in the election of persons process
133 §253.2 Constitutional amendments, §167 Implementation of international law treaties

9.6.2.4 Free committee procedure

Citizens can use their People's Computers to hold private or corporate committees on their own. The Ministry of Digital Affairs offers an option when profiling in the Committee Directory not to specify a state agency as responsible, but to specify persons from the Persons Directory or companies from the Labour Directory. Companies from the various economic zones, residents of cultural protection areas or consumers can use the committee procedure to shape cooperation or coexistence in a direct democratic manner.

9.6.2.5 People's Plenum

The People's Plenum is a one-off committee meeting for individual issues. It is not followed by a voting week. It can be convened at any time for any emerging law by the responsible minister or by the people from a veto quorum of 20% of those entitled to vote.

The People's Plenum is like a small committee. While the entire law is negotiated in the committee and all meetings are conducted with the direct participation of the citizens, the People's Plenum is a one-off meeting in which explosive questions raised by a law or a government decision are clarified with the people. Afterwards, the ministry continues to work on the project on its own.

The Ministry of Foreign Affairs can also hold such events in foreign stadiums in order to negotiate rules together with the other people. The Ministry of Media Affairs is responsible for the organisation.[134]

9.6.2.6 People's Conference

People's Conferences are public press conferences in the street, usually in front of the ministry building or a town hall. Press representatives are allowed to ask one question each first, followed by the citizens. On the panel are responsible

---

134 Ministry of Media Affairs - 7.2.3.6 People's Plenum

politicians, deciders and people in charge of a project that is being realised by a ministry or even partially financed by taxpayers' money.

9.6.2.7 Committees abroad

As soon as the Ministry of Foreign Affairs concludes treaties with a foreign state, the foreign population affected by the domestic state's treaty with their foreign state must agree. The domestic citizens and the foreigner population must agree to the treaty with at least a 65% majority, otherwise the treaty may not be concluded. If a majority is reached abroad, a committee can be held there to amend the treaty accordingly and put it to a final vote. The committee must be held before the international treaties are concluded.

9.6.2.8 Participation of foreigners

Foreigners are also allowed to participate in the committees, to discuss, formulate and propose solutions. But participation in the committee's voting is reserved for those entitled to vote who are nationals. In the medium term, this should be all continental nationals, and in the long term, all citizens of the earth.

9.6.3 Procedure

The process of a committee can vary depending on the type of procedure, but it has certain characteristics that occur in all types of procedures. The ministries of state organisation, media and digital are involved in the procedure. The Ministry of State Organisation takes care of the procedural rules, the Ministry of Media Affairs takes care of the events and the Ministry of Digital Affairs takes care of the broadcast.

9.6.3.1 Preliminary work

Ministries, political parties, affected citizens and the people constantly debate laws and other policies. Ministries do this during their work and in expert panels. Parties do it at party congresses, within party wings and their working groups. Affected citizens do it when they meet in real life or digitally. The people do it on state television and in the directories of the intranet. This is the day-to-day politics. Controversial issues can arise in the process. Contentious issues are characterised by the fact that they are often discussed in opposing ways. Since all political events take place on the intranet, an algorithm can filter out contentious issues and display them to the state media. In the editorial offices, the announcements are checked and included in the reporting. If policies are controversial, a committee is convened. This preliminary work is filmed by Government Television and broadcast before the committee.

9.6.3.2 Convocation[135]

Whether and when a committee must or can be convened is determined by the Ministry of State Organisation in the law on the basis of the relevant constitutional articles.

The constitution provides for committees to formulate constitutional articles and international law treaties. They are convened by the Ministry of State Organisation or the Ministry of Foreign Affairs.

Ministers and citizens are also entitled to convene a committee. Each committee must be assigned to a ministry with primary responsibility. If several ministries are involved in the committee, the Ministry of State Organisation chairs the committee. Federal Moderators are responsible for moderation.

In the case of citizens, however, a veto quorum must be met. At least 30% of the affected citizens must agree for a committee to be convened. Depending on the group of persons affected, committees are convened by affected citizens, municipalities, the people or several peoples.

135§93 Convening of committees

Ministers can convene a committee at any time they deem necessary. As soon as they want to make a decision, they have to publish this will through the state media and then pay attention to the statements of the population. If there is a difference of opinion or a lot of opposition, a minister should convene a committee to make sure that the decision is in the best interest of the population. Ministers can thus pre-empt a veto quorum, repeal quorum or their deselection quorum. However, if ministers want to implement uncontroversial decisions of their majority-supported election platform, an additional unnecessary committee would bore the population and be more conducive to the deselection quorum.

Once convened, the agenda for the committee is set publicly on the intranet and motions and ideas can be expressed by users. The committee must be held no later than 2 weeks after it has been convened.

Guests for the panel can apply in advance on the intranet or be proposed by users. Guests are selected by all users via voting on the intranet and by the politicians involved.

9.6.3.3 Pre-reporting

Pre-reporting takes place one week before the committee. All matters to be decided at the committee must be filmed. The feature films are shown on state television and shows, documentaries and news are broadcast to accompany their content. The films are produced by the Government Television and in the party wings, but they can also be submitted by all citizens.

9.6.3.4 Moving in

Before a committee begins, the People's Motor Vehicle drives at walking pace through the city where the committee is to take place. The People's Motor Vehicles play different music depending on the part of town they are passing through. In the play street children's songs, at the old people's home classical music, on the main street techno, between apartment blocks hip hop and in industrial areas charts. This way, people come to the windows and see what's going on in the street and where the music is coming from. If the citizens feel like it and have time, they follow the dancing crowd and hopefully come along to the rally point. This way, citizens can walk behind the music coming from the outside loudspeakers of the People's Motor Vehicle, just like at the Love Parade[136] . Regular announcements are made as to which ministry and what issue is being discussed in this committee. Every 5 minutes the announcement is made: "Attention, attention, this is the people speaking." On the outside of the glass container, illuminated lettering indicates what the committee is about and how you can participate via your People's Computer. The responsible politicians are already riding in the People's Motor Vehicle and making the announcements. Interested citizens will continue to follow the People's Motor Vehicle. Others who are not interested in the issue will turn back. The trucks with the technology are already at their destination to make all the preparations.

For municipal civic committees, the People's Motor Vehicle travels at 30km/h through the involved localities and changes to walking speed at the entrance to the destination.

National committees are always organised as a star march, so that at least 4 People's Motor Vehicles from all directions slow down to a walking pace 7km before the common central destination. If possible, the PMVs arrive at the assembly point at the same time and take up their positions.

136https://de.wikipedia.org/wiki/Loveparade

In the cities, committees are held on Sundays in the market places, in front of the town halls or in stadiums. Depending on the number of citizens affected, larger venues are chosen. No matter where a committee is held, a coloured helium balloon must float on a coloured rope 500 metres above the committee so that the venue can be found with the naked eye. The People's Motor Vehicle is positioned so that the audience can follow what is happening on the panel and make its contribution. The set-up is described here as an example. In a market place there is a truck with a glass container as a trailer, in which there is an oval table around which the members of the panel sit. At the back above the glass container is a large screen on which the audience can watch the current speaker. Next to the glass container are loudspeakers that transmit the interior sounds. At the front of the glass container, i.e. towards the cab of the Truck, 2 camera cranes are mounted. At the end of these, a camera with spotlights and microphones is mounted on a gimbal.

The smallest committee consists of only one People's Motor Vehicle. The normal committee consists of a People's Motor Vehicle and the two trucks for the technology. In the two technical trucks there is a screen with projector, an inflatable tent roof with water-filled support legs, microphones, cameras and screens for the audience and the control room for the TV broadcast. As soon as the two technical trucks have been emptied, they will be used as a control room and a TV box. The screen will be set up behind the People's Motor Vehicle and the tent roof will be put up in case of rain. Radio microphones and touch screens will be set up in the audience. For national committees, all four PMVs line up in a semicircle and there are more responsible state employees, participants and scientists represented on the panel.

9.6.3.6 Starting ritual

After the welcome and introduction of all guests, all participants should give each other a sign of peace. Similar to the service in the Catholic Church, the moderator speaks the invitation: "Give each other a sign of peace". Then the participants shake hands, each with about 5 persons nearby. This happens both on the panel and in the audience. This gesture is a sign of reconciliation to dedicate the decisions taken at this committee to peace.

9.6.3.7 Media implementation[137]

Committees are broadcast in real time and in full on Government Television, allowing any number of humans to interact and vote regardless of where they are. The Ministry of Media Affairs is responsible for the overall logistical implementation to broadcast the event on the Government Television and Intranet.

---

137 §94 Digital participation in committees

At the front of the container are 4 cranes, as known from some dump trucks. However, here they are used as camera cranes to broadcast the event on state television. In the glass box on the trailer of the People's Motor Vehicle is the panel of responsible politicians, participants and scientists. Microphones are set up in front of the window front, behind which citizens can line up to make their suggestion for improvement. Screens are set up in the crowd to allow people to change the wording of their request in text form using a keyboard.

Anyone who wants to have a say may present something on the topic. Several audience microphones are used to discuss policy issues. The audience members line up one after the other and take their turn. Audience members line up behind the microphones, viewers at the television press the corresponding button on the People's Computer and are shown how many viewers are in front of them. The speaking time is 30 seconds. For a longer speaking time, the audience member must be called to the panel to explain his or her proposal in more detail. The audience microphones have feedback protectors that look like funnels in which the microphones are placed. The discussion is broadcast locally on the screen, on state television and on the intranet.

9.6.3.7.1 TV picture

On the television screen, the state data is displayed in ticker tape at the bottom of the screen. During a voting, they run at the top of the screen and the data is only related to the affected population and its state organs. The affected population, the debt or savings level of the municipality, nation or other level, the unemployment rate of the humans who want to change an economic form but cannot find work there, the birth rate, the suicide rate and the migration balance of inhabitants are displayed. Below that is the picture from the committee's live broadcast. Below that, at the bottom of the screen, there is a belly button with the currently discussed thesis or a current voting question from the panel to the audience, as well as the intranet address as a QR code. The QR code can be scanned with the People's Computer to participate in the solution finding process.

9.6.3.7.2 TV box

Next to the crowd and to the right of the People's Motor Vehicle, the trailer of the truck for the equipment is set up. Two small TV studios are now set up in it, i.e. a room with a camera, spotlight, table, chair and green background. Participants of the committee can go in there to speak their minds, vent frustrations and make suggestions for improvement. There, everyone has 30 seconds to speak and a second chance if their recording is unsuccessful. At the end of the recording, you can watch it again and either upload it or record it again. Afterwards, this recording can also be viewed again and it can be decided whether the first or second video or a compilation should be uploaded or whether one would like to cancel in order to queue up again if necessary.

9.6.3.7.3 Viewers video contributions

The videos uploaded by viewers during the committee or recorded by audience guests in the TV box on the committee appear on the committee's profile page in the Committee Directory.
The page structure is shown here as an example. In the header

is the input bar with the intranet address of the profile page. Below that is the heading "People's votes", next to it a search field, below that "Most viewed" and next to that it is possible to make further settings with a tab. It is possible to switch between displaying the most popular, least popular, newest or oldest videos. The videos are displayed in a filmstrip bar with the video contributions ordered from left to right. As soon as a video contribution is clicked on, the comment history appears below it. Below this are the remits of the ministries to which the video contributions have been assigned by the author. On the right-hand side of the webpage, you can see which videos have been added today. Below that, a tree structure shows which ministry the committee comes from and which issue from which area of the ministry is being dealt with in this committee.

The video view of a single video consists of the following picture elements. You can see the title of the video, video image area, play bar, rating scale with buttons labelled 1,2,3,4,5,6. These buttons are used for users to rate the video. Next to the row of buttons, the average score is displayed with one decimal place. Below the row of buttons, a small bar chart is displayed that shows the grade level. Under each button, the percentage of the ratings that have fallen on this grade so far is displayed. Next to it is the total number of votes cast. Below that is a comment bar.

This way, all posted videos are displayed when they are clicked. The rating tool from 1 to 6 can also be switched again by the creator of the video via the comment bar. This allows the creator to add a poll to their video. The creator assigns a title for the poll and has 200 characters for the question. Viewers can then choose between, for example, 6 proposals, i.e. type 1 for more co-determination, 2 for less co-determination, 3 for national co-determination, 4 for municipal co-determination, 5 for no co-determination at all, 6 for other and that is [Free input field].

9.6.3.7.4 Video competition

The top 10 most viewed and rated videos will be discussed with the affected members of the panel and audience during the broadcast of the committee. For this purpose, the videos will be broadcast on the video wall behind the People's Motor Vehicle and on state television. The profits will be invited to the panel for a short discussion with panel members and questions from the audience.

9.6.3.8 Motivation during the committee

To motivate and cheer up the participants involved, there is a time of joy lasting about 30 seconds. All voluntary participants can rejoice like children rejoice. The panel moderator asks the question: "Are you happy?" once agreement has been reached. Then there are shouts of joy, laughter and bouncing as long as music is played.

9.6.3.9 Voting during the committee

To vote, all participants will receive their voting cards next to the People's Motor Vehicle. Those who have brought their People's Computer themselves will not receive voting cards. Viewers at the televisions can use their People's Computers as voting remote controls. The voting options of the solution inventors apply.[x] The voting cards will be printed with a new QR code for each committee in a chip card printer. The cards are reusable and can be purchased by citizens, kept and brought or collected again and again. For free use, participants can get a voting card, hand in the purchase price as a deposit, return it after leaving the committee and get their deposit money back. Each participant receives a red and a green voting card. They both have a QR code in the top half, which contains the information written down below. In the lower half is the name of the citizen to whom the voting card is issued. Below that is the organiser, which can be a ministry, several ministries, a party or a party wing, the sequence number of the total committees held, the date and the location.

When the panel or the audience calls for a majority vote, the cards are held up and scanned overhead at an angle from the top of the stage with a camera from the edge of the stage to the last row of the audience. When doing this, the voting card must be held with the fingers on the writing and not on the QR code.

At the same time, viewers at the televisions can press the corresponding button via their People's Computer. Participants in the committee may also be asked to bring their People's Computers to replace the voting cards.

9.6.3.10 Secret voting during the committee

During secret ballots, citizens should make sure that they cannot be observed while voting with their People's Computer. At meetings with the People's Motor Vehicle, all citizens should look down to the ground, cover their eyes with one hand and only then hold their voting card up with the other hand. The cameras scan the voting cards, but do not broadcast the image on state television, instead broadcasting a still image with the voting question while they do so. As soon as the voting result is known, a beep sounds and the participants can read the result on the screen.

9.6.3.11 End

When the list of concerns has been worked through and all deciders have been made, dance music is played. The DJ or band plays from the moderator's cue. The cue is "Feierabend!" The closing ritual is to sing the national anthem together while everyone holds hands. During the anthem, even strangers should shake hands and hold them for the duration of the national anthem. No human should stand alone, but be connected to the entire crowd by at least one hand. Circles should be avoided. After the national anthem, all those who have been holding hands should place both hands on the shoulders of their left-hand neighbour and form a polonaise. To a closing song, the polonaise is danced and anyone who now wants to leave can leave the polonaise at the appropriate outside point of the crowd.

9.6.4 Committee Directory

Each committee receives a profile in the Committee Directory. The profile is also the intranet page of a committee. Users can submit proposals, comment on them and rate them. During committees on government decisions and legislative processes, the profile is linked to the corresponding profile in the Legislative Directory. After the committee, the link is made to the elected politician's profile in the Labour Directory or to the decision passed in the Law Directory.
On the profile, all Committee video recordings are made accessible via links to the Media Directory[138] . Groups in the Committee Directory can be formed from all those who attend or have attended a committee in person.

9.6.5 Venues[139]

Committees can last for several days of hearings or have already reached their goal after one event. No matter how many dates there are, events can be held in several places at the same time on one date or only in one place. The venue is located where citizens show increased interest in the topic. In order to have a committee held at several locations, the People's Motor Vehicle is used. For example, there are employees of an opencast mine for lignite and residents who are to be resettled. Then there is a People's Motor Vehicle at the opencast mine with the employees and a second People's Motor Vehicle in the centre of the village.
The aim is for committees to be held in places where the attitudes of the citizens living there towards the matter under discussion differ as much as possible. Who has a favourable or unfavourable attitude is captured by different data. Firstly, the number of party members who are in a party wing in

---

138 Ministry of Media Affairs - 5.6 Media Directory
139 §79,5,6 Venues

the specified area that indicates a relevant stance in favour or against in its basic programme and working groups is recorded. Secondly, all statements, ratings and votes of users on the issue on the intranet are analysed for favourable or unfavourable statements and categorised by place of residence. Thirdly, past voting results on a similar issue are recorded. Fourthly, demonstrations, petitions and initiatives and their attitude towards the issue are listed. All data is related to the users' place of residence. The resulting map differs in colour. The colour scale shows in which place how many citizens have a favourable or unfavourable attitude. In light red areas, few citizens have a negative attitude. The opposite is true for dark red areas. In dark green areas, many citizens have a favourable attitude. In light green areas, the opposite is true. If the divergence is very strong, several committees will have to be held simultaneously through video conferencing at several locations. The panelists are invited to the locations where the local population does not share the same opinion, depending on their stance.

Committees should rotate in their area of operation. A municipality consisting of only one neighbourhood or village is the smallest unit and does not need to rotate. However, if the decisions of the committee affect several towns or districts, the committee must be held in several places. How long a decision takes depends on the matter being decided. Usually, a matter should not be discussed for more than one day. If no agreement is reached, all those present and watching are asked how the matter should proceed. Through this survey, majorities emerge on the map. A distinction is made between citizens who reject the request, those who support it or those who still want to change it in order to support it. Now the three cities in which majorities in one of the camps have formed are selected as target cities. For example, in the city of Berlin there would be a majority in favour of adopting a proposed law, but in the town of Buxtehude there would be a majority against and in Augsburg there would be a majority in favour of changing the proposed law. Then this national committee would be held in Berlin, Buxtehude and Augsburg. Apart from that, committees move around the country on a scheduled basis so that each town hall announces when the next committee will be in that town and which ministry is hosting it. The aim is to hold committees all over the country and not only in big cities or the capital cities of the ministries. Cities are targeted, regardless of their size, which are once for and once against a concern, or represent negative or positive examples of a particular concern. Here, proposals can be made in advance on the intranet and voted on by the users.

9.6.6 Support

Mobile toilet containers are set up around the committee and are lent out by the disaster management. Municipal catering establishments are allowed to set up around the committee. At national committees, there are additional supply containers where food from the Social Market Economy and Planned Economy is offered at shop prices. Retail businesses from the Social Market Economy and Planned Economy can participate in the national tender. Either the tender takes place every 2 years or is re-tendered after a veto quorum of the customers. The rating is based on the best price-performance ratio. The aim is to attract as many humans as possible to the committee and to offer the stay as cheaply as possible. For this, there is the exclusive contract with the retail company that won the tender.
The goods may not be sold at a higher price than in the shop, even if they are smaller containers. For example, a six-pack of beer costs the same in the shop as six bottles sold individually at the committee.

9.6.7 Party advertising

At committee meetings there are always motions to join a party. Each party member should indicate his or her political views and expertise on this form. All parties are allowed to recruit members. Anyone may join as many parties as they wish. Those who can speak and argue well at a committee are more likely to be recruited specifically by parties.

9.7 Voting[140]

In voting, citizens determine how their state deals with them. All state decisions are only in the best interests of the people and in accordance with the will of the voters if they have been voted on. Voting is held during an election week to give all those entitled to vote sufficient time to visit the voting computers.

When votes are due, they are held by the humans who are affected by them. Those affected citizens of a state, citizens of a municipality, the people of a nation or peoples of several nations may be entitled to vote.

Voting takes place whenever politicians, citizens or the constitution require it. This may be the case when ministers wish to have a government decision scrutinised before it is implemented. If an appropriate quorum is triggered, voting can also take place directly. At the end of a committee, a voting is always held to confirm the text developed.

Voting on state decisions of the past year takes place at the latest during the annual budget vote. This happens in three ways. First, when a majority approval vote approves the government's policies and confirms the politicians in office for the past year. Second, when the distribution of state revenues among the ministries and their projects is decided. Thirdly, when the legislative packages of the individual ministries are approved or rejected in a legislative vote.

If citizens do not decide otherwise, indirect democracy applies and ministries have a quorum if ministers are present. If citizens determine direct democracy through a veto quorum or participation quorum, the citizens have a quorum. If citizens determine representative democracy, the councils of ministers have a quorum if all deputy ministers are present. If citizens lend out their vote to party members, party councils are quorate when all delegates are present.

As soon as small votes in committees are necessary to decide negotiation channels, at least 5% of those entitled to vote must be present.

Personal presence in the building or digital presence via digital devices of the intranet does not play a role, as long as all

---

140§86 Voting, §80 Negotiators and quorum

necessary persons are present at the same time. Motions must be submitted in real form at the town hall or digitally on the intranet before the meeting.

9.7.1 Three ways of voting

Voting takes place at the conclusion of the election of persons and legislation procedures. Whether these Negotiations were direct, indirect or representative, the voting procedure can again be direct, indirect or representative. Citizens can vote directly in the election week, delegates indirectly in the party council or councillors representatively in the responsible council.

9.7.2 Preventing electoral fraud

Citizens can vote in all town halls as long as they have their identity card with them. They must expel their identity card into the voting computer and have their palm print and iris scanned to avoid multiple voting.

Citizens are protected against electoral fraud by issuing two receipts. The receipt is issued to the citizen either in paper form or as an entry in the People's Computer. A receipt roll is printed in the town hall, which is getting fuller and fuller. After his election, each voter can only see his own line through a small window as he voted. As soon as he leaves the voting booth, the receipt roll rotates one line further.

9.7.3 Majorities[141]

Votes shall be deemed adopted if a majority of 65% has voted in favour and at least 30% of those entitled to vote have participated in the voting. They shall be deemed rejected if a majority has voted against. The majority ratios are expressed as a percentage. They correspond to the percentage of those entitled to vote, i.e. how many of those entitled to vote were in favour and against. The missing percentages indicate the

---

141 §81 Majorities required: BV Art.142, §80 Negotiators and Quorum

number of non-voters. Thus, voting results always contain the turnout, supporters and opponents of a decision.

Those entitled to vote can decide for themselves when the majority is reached. It must be at least above 50% of the votes cast. The percentage majority required for a vote to be considered adopted is determined by those entitled to vote by a majority of 65%. If these majority ratios are to be changed, a majority quorum must be met.

The quorum for direct democratic procedures is reached as soon as 30% of those entitled to vote cast their vote in a repeal quorum or veto quorum. The affected state decider is then negotiated in a committee. The 30% number can be changed by the citizens via the quorum limits quorum.

In the representative procedures, 40% of the responsible council members must be against a decision by the minister for the decision to be negotiated in the responsible council. In the following voting, at least 65% of the councillors must agree for it to be carried out. Citizens can change these percentages through a majority quorum.

9.7.3.1 Municipal majorities

If a municipality administers itself, the majorities of those entitled to vote only apply in that municipality. For example, if a vote has been held in the whole country and there are 40% against and 60% in favour, but in a self-administered municipality there is a majority of those who voted against, the vote in the municipality is considered rejected. The votes cast are evaluated for the individual municipalities. The majority ratios in this separate count are binding for the voting. Votes can thus be rejected on a municipal basis, even though they were approved nationally. Even if the municipality does not administer itself, the results are published as to how the citizens of a municipality voted. Voting computers record where people live when they vote and the counts run automatically for the individual municipalities and the national or even international level.

This allows citizens to see whether it is worth administering themselves and whether they should seek a subsidiarity vote for the ministry in question. If a municipality's voting behaviour differs significantly from national or international voting behaviour several times, then the municipality should administer itself. But if the voting pattern is the same, then self-government should be abandoned or not introduced at all. Instead, a municipal law can be enacted to introduce an exception.

9.7.4 Mandatory voting[142]

The people must vote on constitutional articles, laws and international law or treaties. If laws or international treaties are rejected, they must be negotiated in a committee, if this has not already been done. If this has already been done, they are considered to have been definitively rejected.

If laws are declared urgent by the responsible politician to apply immediately, the voting public votes on them within 7 days in an election week. In cases of particular urgency, the immediate voting may be held within 24 hours for a period of 24 hours. If the voting is accepted, it can only be annulled or reversed by a repeal quorum.

If money is to be paid that was not approved in the previous budget vote, it must be voted on beforehand.

9.7.5 Binding coordination topics[143]

Certain policies have to be made by the affected citizens and cannot be negotiated or voted on in a representative way by politicians.

9.7.5.1 Peoples

All long-term decisions that affect several peoples must be voted on by all citizens of all affected states. These are accessions or exits to international organisations, such as the

---

142 §253,2 Constitutional amendments: BV Art.192, §167
Implementation of international law treaties: BV Art. 141a
143 §87 Mandatory referendums: BV Art.140, KV Art.61

United Nations[144] , the North Atlantic Treaty Organisation (NATO) or the Continental Union. All these organisations are in a position to impose rules on the legislative power of the state and can thereby subvert the will of the people. Whether the regulations correspond to the will of the participating peoples can only be found out by voting among all affected citizens. Citizens must be clear about the financial, legal or life-threatening obligations they are entering into by participating in an international organisation. They must be able to join or leave an international organisation at any time by a majority of 65%.

All international treaties concluded between two, more or all states must first be approved by 65% of the affected citizens of all participating peoples. This rule also applies to trade agreements. Negotiations for such treaties must be conducted in public and their contents must be made fully available to those entitled to vote in the form of digital text files on the internet, intranet and town halls. Prior to voting during an election week, the draft agreements must have been filmed and broadcast on state television.

As soon as the national territory is to be changed, all citizens of all states affected by the change of their external borders must vote on it. From a majority of 65% in all affected peoples, the border shift is permissible.

9.7.5.2 People

Certain politicians' decisions affect the people as a nation, but not other states. In order for such deciders to take effect, the people must approve them by a majority of 65%. These are amendments to the constitution necessitated by court judgments or proposed legislation, as well as constitutional initiatives for a total or partial amendment of individual or all constitutional articles.

This is the change to the territories of all municipalities. Boundary corrections of adjoining territories of neighbouring municipalities are excluded.

This is the conclusion of treaties between municipalities that

---

144https://www.un.org/en/

contradict at least one constitutional article in whole or in part.

This is the annual voting on the budget of all nationally administered ministries for the coming year.

This is the annual voting on all laws that are to apply nationwide from the coming year. This does not include laws that have already been voted on by the people in the year of legislation, such as laws declared urgent.

These are the votes in the event of war, which are to decide every three months whether to go to war or surrender.

This is the voting on whether an international treaty should be drafted by responsible ministries or in a committee.

This is the voting on whether state property should be sold, closed down or privatised, where the proceeds or losses should go or how to further deal with the affected state property.

These are urgently declared laws that have no constitutional basis and must be voted on before they come into force.

This also includes any policy or initiative that has been declared compulsory by a quorum or committee.

9.7.6 Annual budget vote[145]

As the only exception to elections and voting according to a quorum, the periodic budget vote[146] is held annually. The reason for this is that the revenues and expenditures of the state must be continuously adjusted in order to set contemporary priorities. If possible, all other election and voting dates are also set to coincide with this periodic vote, if citizen participation would otherwise be lower and if too many programmes for elections of persons do not then need to be known by the citizens. A flood of information must be avoided at all costs so that citizens can exercise their right to vote appropriately in addition to their daily lives.

In the dynamic media democracy, the people have the right to determine their own tax resources. To this end, the ministries of state organisation, finance, intranet and media work together to offer the citizens this opportunity. In this way, all

---

145§46.3 State
146Ministry of Finance - 9.5 Budget vote

politicians vote with the population on the amount of taxes and how they are to be spent each year.

Every year, the people distribute the national budget for the coming year in the budget vote. The Ministry of Finance is responsible for its implementation.[147] The Ministry of State Organisation regulates the political processes, which are similar to the legislative process. At the beginning, each ministry prepares a draft, the So-called financial plan. Then, in voting with all ministries, the Ministry of Finance combines their financial plans into the draft budget. The draft budget is worked out in a budget committee to form the budget bill. This is followed by an election campaign and an election week for the budget vote.

Citizens also vote on this occasion to approve the discharge of governments for the past year. Pre-elections of persons also fall on this day so that candidates for new programmes can also advertise for tax money at the same time to implement them. On this election date, all new laws or deletions of the past year are also listed and can be approved or rejected individually.

9.7.6.1 Approval vote

In the approval vote, citizens vote on the sum total of all decisions made by governments in the past year. This applies to the entire ministries. Individual government decisions and responsible politicians, state employees or entire ministries can be selected not to be approved. The votes go into the deselection quorum of the selected politicians, the dismissal quorum of the state employees, and the empowerment quorum of the ministry, respectively. If a majority of 60% has not approved the entire ministry, popular empowerment takes place. After the approval vote is passed, the liability passes from the politicians to those entitled to vote.

---

147 Ministry of Finance - 9 State expenditure

9.7.6.2 Legislative vote[148]

In the legislative vote, all individual laws that were enacted in the past year but have not yet been voted on are voted on as a package. Laws that are presented to those entitled to vote in a package must also be able to be voted on individually. It is also possible to include other packages of laws in a ministry's legislative package. In this way, all the necessary laws for a reform project can be combined, or even if several ministries were involved. Here, too, it must be possible to open the packages in the voting in order to accept or reject all individual laws.

All rejected laws of a ministry are negotiated in committees, if the responsible minister insists or if the rejecting majority was not clear enough. If 30 to 50% of the voters do not confirm a law, this law is then negotiated in a committee. This can be the case with several laws. They are then negotiated in individual committees during the course of the year. The responsible ministers agree on a schedule, on which date which law is to be negotiated.

If laws are then rejected again, they may not be introduced a third time. Laws that have been supported by a vote are valid immediately after the vote.

9.7.7 Public financing by the Central Bank

The state is only allowed to take on debts in order to establish a new natural monopoly. Natural monopolies are companies that require a very high initial investment with immense fixed costs. Once this infrastructure is in place, the cost of another unit being produced or supported is vanishingly small. Examples of this are the railways or the telecommunications network. Whether one passenger rides more or less is of little consequence, as is supporting one mobile phone more or less. Government financing by banks or other creditors, especially from abroad, is inadmissible. Only the democratically elected head of the Central Bank is responsible for lending to the citizens and politicians. Only he may borrow money from the

---

148§75,2 Legislation: BV Art.51

population or fire up the printing press to print new money and increase the money supply, thereby devaluing existing money.

Every minister is entitled to ask the people for a loan. 75% of the affected population must agree. The credit may only be granted by these affected citizens. If 75% of the entire people agree, the credit balances on the current accounts of the bank accounts at the People's Bank[149] are used for the investment. However, the amount of money available in the current account will remain the same for People's Bank clients. All the money that People's Bank customers withdraw at this time is put back into circulation by the Central Bank. This financing by the Central Bank increases the money supply. In the long run, this expropriates all those who hold this currency. Therefore, the Central Bank has to keep accurate records of how much money it has spent. These banknotes have to be reprinted and dispensed from ATMs. The money supply is gradually paid back to the monetary cycle from the profits of the new natural monopolies. To the same extent, banknotes must immediately be withdrawn from the cash cycle again.

If the state goes into debt with its citizens, this must be negotiated in a committee. All plans and costs must be made public. Citizens can suggest how the concept could be more cost-effective or innovative.

The ballot paper contains the question: Should <u>the state take out</u> a loan for <u>this project</u>? A tick can now be placed behind "Yes" or behind "No". The two underlined parts of the sentence are linked, so that under "the state" you can see which politician in which ministry is responsible for this at which level. Under "this project" is the entire project description including all cost statements and cost estimates. All voters have the opportunity here to rate individual or several cost items as "unnecessary" or "too high". The responsible politician does not sign the purchase contracts until after the voting. If clear doubts become apparent during the voting, the politician can review them, extend the committee if necessary, and hold another vote.

Under the voting question, there is the option of placing a tick

---

149Ministry of Finance - 11 People's Bank

next to "deselection" to vote out the responsible politician(s). A link to the quorum of the responsible politician follows. If more than one politician is involved, you first have to specify which behaviour is considered to be incorrect. Then the appropriate politicians are available for selection. Multiple voting is possible. Now the voter can add his vote for the deselection quorum to each politician's name by ticking the box.

9.7.8 Privatisation and nationalisation of companies

If a state enterprise is to be privatised, the affected population must agree. For example, in the case of local utilities, only the citizens of the city or municipality that is affected vote. State-owned companies operating nationwide or worldwide and People's Innovation Company[150] without valid patent protection require 65% approval by the people to be sold.
Insofar as a private enterprise is to be nationalised, this enterprise must either be insolvent or of nationwide importance. When citizens unite as a people in order to secure basic needs for all affected citizens and provide for them themselves or place them in the hands of municipal or national administration, this creates popular relevance. The majority ratios here are 75% of the people.
Both procedures have to be negotiated in a People's Committee, because this is about buying or selling prices of people's property. If the purchase prices are too high or the sale prices too low, the people can end the negotiations at any time.

9.7.9 Politicians' salaries

Politicians' salaries are assessed by the affected population. The citizens set a capitation fee. It is asked how much each citizen would be willing to pay monthly for the politician. The amount can be entered in the voting window and the politician's monthly salary is automatically displayed in a field

---

150 Ministry of Innovation - 10 People's Innovation Company

next to it. The algorithm recognises which citizens are affected by a politician and adds up the result. The user can change the amount as often as desired to see what the salary would be if all those entitled to vote indicated this capitation rate. The algorithm now uses the median to calculate the politician's salary. The amount of money that was given most often by all citizens is paid out.

Salaries are Tax-funded, so a tax increase or decrease may result from a salary adjustment. The determination is made annually for the budget vote. Politicians can additionally submit a motion for a salary increase at least 4 weeks before the voting. The salary is the price for the politician's work. As with all prices of the state, 10% profits are added, which go directly into the ministry's coffers.

9.8 State governments[151]

The government of the state forms the executive, i.e. the executive state powers. A government is formed for each individual case. The individual case decides which ministries are responsible to meet a policy challenge. The 18 different ministries offer a wide range of remits to allocate responsibilities. Ministries govern independently in the area of accountability of their ministry if they do not have to cooperate with other ministers in an individual case.

Citizens can be involved in government through the same procedures as in the legislature. In the election of persons, those entitled to vote decide on the programme of government and the candidates for government. Government decisions are made directly, indirectly or representatively by the citizens.

The normal case is indirect government, in which directly elected ministers make government decisions in voting with the ministry's staff and thus plan, coordinate and execute its activities. If ministers have to make a government decision immediately in a dangerous situation that is not regulated by a law, the state of exception occurs and the Council of Exception convenes.

151§104,1-4 Government decisions, §103,1 Government policy BV Art.180

The exceptional case is direct government, where citizens partially intervene in the planning, coordination and deciding of the government through committees and voting. Outright intervention allows citizens to usurp any governmental functions of a ministry through the process of popular empowerment.

The special case is representative government, in which all directly elected deputy ministers of a ministry make government decisions in the Council of Ministers.

Either the minister decides independently which case enters or the citizens decide by triggering a corresponding quorum. Through the veto quorum, a pending government decision is put to a vote or negotiated beforehand in a committee. Through the participation quorum, government decisions of a ministry are permanently taken directly, indirectly or representatively. The repeal quorum puts an existing government decision to a vote or negotiates it in a committee beforehand.

9.8.1 Government decisions[152]

Government decisions are laws, ordinances, municipal laws, statutes, administrative instructions or service instructions. While laws and municipal laws come into being after the legislative process and must always be voted on by the affected citizens, this is only provided for in exceptional cases in the case of ordinances, statutes, administrative instructions or service instructions. Government decisions can affect a group of people, a municipality, a group of municipalities, several municipalities, a nation or several nations. Citizens who are affected are given voting rights for quorums, committees and votes. Politicians who are affected are the directly elected international, national, municipal or deputy ministers. The Ministry of Foreign Affairs is responsible for international government decisions and encourages citizen participation through membership in International Unions.[153]

152§104.5,6 Government decisions
153Ministry of Foreign Affairs - 5 Communitarisation

9.8.2 Responsibility[154]

The people are responsible for giving the government a constitution under which it may lawfully make deciders. The people monitor the exercise through the state media and the intranet. Citizens have the right to appeal to the Constitutional Court at any time against an allegedly unconstitutional state action.

Citizens are voluntary members of parties according to their interests and assign themselves to party wings. Party members can stand for election to a ministerial post. Citizens determine the timing of new elections through the deselection quorum and make choices between programmes and candidates. They elect one minister for each of the 18 ministries in separate ballots.

Ministers and their deputies have the responsibility to oversee the administration of the ministry and its state or private executing agencies.

The Ministry of State Organisation assumes responsibility for chairing, moderating and mediating when several ministries are involved in the government in an individual case. If no agreement can be reached, the responsible Federal Moderator convenes a committee.

9.8.2.1 Ministers in government[155]

The government consists of at least one and up to 18 directly elected ministers. As a rule, only one ministry is responsible for a government decision. Responsible ministers act independently and alone form the government for all these individual cases. Governing ministers decide on their own authority whether to involve other persons, politicians, ministries, councils of ministers, party councils or committees in the government.

Each minister governs his ministry heterarchically together with all responsible staff. The responsible staff are experts in

---

154§106,1-3 Responsibility for government and control, §107,1a,2,3
Powers of governments: BV Art.173
155§108 Composition and election of the government: BV Art.175

the specific service delivery and work with the minister on the best possible course of action to implement the will of the people. Services that are provided differently at the municipal level are planned and coordinated by the deputy ministers in their municipality with the ministry staff there.

Citizens monitor persons in government through the deselection quorum and the subsequent direct election of ministers and their government programmes. Citizens monitor government decisions through the veto quorum and the repeal quorum. They can submit Counter-drafts through the initiative quorum or choose between the direct, indirect or representative way of decision-making through the participation quorum.

9.8.2.2 Cooperation between several ministries[156]

The individual case determines how many ministries would be affected by the government decision if it were implemented. If several ministries are affected, ministers or citizens report in a veto quorum. The Ministry of State Organisation examines the reports. All affected ministries are involved in the government for this individual case. The Federal Moderator's Office takes the chair and Federal Moderators moderate the government process.

In principle, ministers report to their ministry, unless responsibility lies with several ministries. In cabinet meetings, ministers discuss interdepartmental laws together with other ministers and the Federal Moderator. In the case of a state service, the responsible employees from the ministry who are later to provide this service are invited to the committee or council. In the case of a law that does not result in a state service involving employees of the ministry, party members from the party wings who have the most expertise are invited. If there is a disagreement in the joint execution of laws between several ministries, a Federal Moderator takes the final decision or convenes a committee.

156§109 Chair of the government: BV Art.176

9.8.2.3 Collegial principle[157]

If several ministries work together in a governmental procedure, the collegial principle applies. It means that ministers distribute tasks and make decisions unanimously as a collegiate body. It also means that in each ministry, politicians and workers work together to implement the will of the people and the laws according to the heterarchical principle of organisation.

If the phrase ''...in voting with...'' is found in laws or constitutional articles, all participants have equal voting rights. In the case of equal majority ratios, the circle of those entitled to vote is expanded. First, all the elected politicians involved are called upon. First comes the moderating Federal Moderator. He can use his vote to decide the majority, try to negotiate further, give voting rights to even more staff of the affected ministries or hold a public interactive negotiation on state television.

Every government and its executive state organs are bound by the will of the people, the constitution and the laws and must act within this prescribed scope of action. In order to be able to effectively control this principle, all government negotiations must be broadcast simultaneously on state television and permanently published on the intranet.[158]

9.8.3 Control[159]

Citizens must be informed about all government decisions in a timely manner, i.e. from the conception of ideas, and comprehensively, i.e. with all information that is also available to the government. This information must be made available to all citizens without delay, at any time and for an unlimited period, and it must be possible to comment on and evaluate it. This is ensured by the ministries for media and digital affairs. In addition, the state television, together with the

---

157 §110 Collegial principle: BV Art.177
158 Ministry of Media - 7 Government Television: for national and international negotiations, 9 Local Television: for municipal negotiations, 5.6 Media Directory
159 §106.5-9 Responsibility for government and control, §103.2
Government policy: BV Art.180, §107.1b-d Powers of governments

Party Television and Surveillance Television, ensures regular reporting on the management of all ministries and the state of the country. The state of the country is captured through all state statistical data, audits by the Company Auditing Agency, and investigations and reports by the state and private press, and published by state television. Reporting focuses on one or more municipalities or nations, depending on the government's area of accountability.

Complaints from citizens are recorded by the Federal Moderator's Office and forwarded to the responsible body. The Internal Service and the External Service decide on the individual procedural channels.

Citizens control the government by following government action on state television and in the Legislative Directory. The ministries of media and digital provide opportunities for participation. State television offers interviews during shows and after reports or feature films. The Legislative Directory allows users to publish and negotiate their own issues and proposals in government decision profiles.

As soon as a sufficient number of citizens cast their vote for one of the following quorums, a committee is convened by the Ministry of State Organisation and, if so decided in the committee, a vote is held. In the case of the veto quorum, a committee is convened while the government is still in session. In the case of a repeal quorum, government decisions that have been adopted are repealed by voting or renegotiated in a committee and, if necessary, reissued in an amended form. In the deselection quorum, positions and programmes of governing persons are re-elected. When voting on the deselection quorum, those entitled to vote may use the questionnaire to justify their dislike. Those entitled to vote have one vote per term of a politician.

Once enough citizens cast their votes for one of the following three options during the budget vote, government decisions become ineffective and can be renegotiated in a committee. First, if the government decision incurs costs, those entitled to vote can cancel that budget item for the coming year. Second, if responsible ministers are not approved, a new election is automatically held. The following government decisions are then tied to a new programme. Existing government decisions of the previous year can be reversed. There is no liability on the part of the state for damage. Exceptions to this are government decisions with immediate voting. Thirdly, government decisions in the form of laws must be accepted or rejected by the citizens in a voting. Government decisions in any other form are effective immediately upon enactment by the responsible ministers.

Citizens elect the deputy ministers responsible for the municipality where the voters live. Government decisions can thus be adapted to local conditions and observed by the local population and rated by voting or determined by committee.

9.8.4 Liability[160]

Politicians in office are liable with their deselection quorum if they do not implement the will of the people. If politicians or state organs subordinate to them unlawfully cause damage in the course of their official activities, the originators are personally liable under civil and criminal law. All claims over and above this are borne by the state treasury. Employees in the state service and politicians can take out insurance. The Ministry of State Organisation manages this liability insurance.

The state is liable for all government decisions once they have been voted on. The state consists of the nation and municipalities. Votes that transfer liability from the governing politicians to those entitled to vote take place either as the conclusion of the decision-making process or as part of the annual budget vote. On this date, all the laws of the previous year are voted on in the legislative ballot. All other decisions by politicians and their ministries are voted on at the same time in the approval vote.

In the case of municipal government decisions, the responsible municipal politicians are liable prior to voting. If a national government decision is implemented locally or factually

---

160§105 Liability for government decisions, §106.9 Responsibility for government and control

adapted by a deputy minister, the deputy minister is liable only for the damage in his or her municipality. If the affected ministry is administered municipally itself, the municipal minister is liable. After voting, those voting are liable as a municipality.

In the case of national government decisions affecting the whole country, the responsible ministers are liable as a nation before the voting and the voting members after the voting. In the case of international government decisions, the member states are liable separately until the ministry affected is led by an international minister. Liability damages are paid from the budget of the affected ministry and may not affect other ministries that are not communitarised.

9.8.5 Administration[161]

The administration, that is all executive functional organisations through which the government carries out the purposeful fulfilment of its tasks. How the government may proceed in doing so is described in the following administrative procedure law. A ministry, headed by a minister, is responsible for the administration of each politician's remit. The administration is federally divided into the international, national and municipal levels. When the administration is responsible for which level is decided by the citizens in a subsidiarity vote.

The administration is divided into departments and agencies within the ministries. The departments or agencies may be headed by directly elected politicians if the citizens so determine according to a staff quorum.

All tasks of the administration are digitised by the Ministry of Digital Affairs and published together with the Ministry of Media Affairs for the affected citizens on state television. Exceptions apply only to the protection of personal data, which cannot be anonymised.

The administration is at the service of the people to fulfil its constitutional tasks. The tasks are described more precisely by the ministers through laws and responsible politicians through other norms. Audit services and citizens control compliance

---

161 §111 Administration: BV Art.178, KV Art.95

with the requirements. In order to be able to effectively carry out this control, directly elected politicians are authorised to issue instructions to administrative staff. As soon as disagreements arise between ministry staff and politicians or ministers, or disagreements arise in the joint administration of several ministries, the Internal Service of the Federal Ministry of the Interior clarifies the discrepancies. The Internal Service then first clarifies which administration should assume which responsibilities in the procedure and coordinates its vote with the politicians and staff responsible. Any harmonisation projects that arise in the process are moderated by the Internal Service and compliance with them is monitored.

Ministers may establish or close departments, authorities, organisations or companies within their ministry. The organisations and companies can be state or privately run. State participation in private organisations or companies is possible, as is the transfer of state tasks to private persons, organisations or companies. Citizens are given an opportunity to object through the veto quorum or repeal quorum.

Any transfer or involvement of administrative tasks must be regulated by law. Tasks that restrict fundamental rights, levy taxes or fees cannot be transferred to private organisations or companies. The law must at least describe how the departments, authorities, state or private organisations and companies organise and perform their tasks. Should the administration be allowed to issue norms below the level of regulations, ministers or responsible politicians must lend out this right to the administration through a law.

State and private agencies carrying out tasks by which government decisions are administered are subject to the supervision of the ministry for which they work. The responsibility for the performance of tasks by the administration lies with the responsible ministers or politicians of the ministry.

9.9 Elections of persons[162]

The people elect the national politicians and the affected citizens elect the municipal politicians. Which government personnel are directly elected is determined by the citizens who are affected by the policies of the personnel to be elected. Committees are responsible for selecting candidates and their policy programmes to be put to the vote of those entitled to vote. The party wings draw up programmes and send the candidates. The programme committee determines which programmes are to be combined. It presents its results to those entitled to vote for the run-off election. The candidates' committee prepares the run-off election by selecting two candidates per programme to run against each other.

In the election of persons, the qualifications and programme of a candidate for a state service position are verified by those eligible to vote. Directly elected state personnel are called politicians. These are international, national or municipal ministers, deputy ministers in all municipalities, and directly elected senior staff of a ministry at international, national or municipal level.

The Ministry of State Organisation is responsible for the regularisation and coordination of the electoral process. In particular, if voting rights are to apply only to affected citizens in an election of persons, this affectedness must be voted on and confirmed by the people beforehand. The Ministry of Media Affairs conducts the events and broadcasts them on state television so that viewers can interactively participate in the event via their People's Computers. The ministries of media and digital affairs ensure interactive implementation, preparation and follow-up as well as the archiving of all data from the events.

---

162 §59 Politicians, §61 Election of persons process

9.9.1 Election advertising

Parties are allowed to advertise on state television to have their minister new elected so that a different programme can be implemented.[163] The free advertising minutes are divided equally among all party wings by the party leader. Each party is allocated the same number of advertising minutes. In this way, opposing party wings can try to drive the deselection quorum of their party's minister to fulfilment through television advertising.

9.9.2 Term of office[164]

The new election takes place as soon as a politician has been deselected by the deselection quorum. This happens when the number of votes in the deselection quorum reaches the number of votes that elected a politician to office. All those entitled to vote have one vote for a politician's deselection quorum for each term of office. Whether and when those entitled to vote want to deselect politicians is not restricted by a time limit. Politicians may stand for re-election provided there are at least 2 other applicants and they have not been criminally convicted while in office.

9.9.3 Incompatibilities[165]

Politicians cannot simultaneously hold several offices for which they must be elected. Politicians must suspend or lend out any other gainful employment for their term of office. There is a right to termination without notice of any gainful employment because of election to political office. Companies owned by politicians before the election may be transferred to relatives for the term of office or administered as state enterprises in trust by the Ministry of Labour. The profits to be distributed go 80% to the politician and 20% to the state treasury.

---

163 Ministry of Media Affairs - 5.3 Advertising
164 §63 Term of office: BV Art.145
165 §62 Incompatibilities: BV Art.144

9.9.4 Procedure[166]

Within 2 months of meeting the deselection quorum, there must be pre-elections, within 4 months run-off elections.

9.9.4.1 Triggering the new election

As soon as the deselection quorum has been triggered, a politician resigns or a majority of councillors support a vote of no confidence, the election of persons procedure begins. The deselection quorum is deemed to be fulfilled as soon as a sufficient number of those entitled to vote have cast their vote for the deselection of the affected politician. The sufficient number of those entitled to vote is fulfilled as soon as the number of votes has been reached that had elected the affected politician to office in his or her last election of persons. In the case of councillors, a majority of 55% must be reached.

9.9.4.2 Transition phase

The affected politician remains in office until the new election is completed and the newly elected politician has been inducted. During this transition period, the deselection quorum for the incumbent politician continues to run. If the deselection quorum rises above 90% of those entitled to vote, the incumbent politician must resign immediately. A Federal Moderator, who is familiar with the work of the affected ministry, takes over during the transition period. The enactment of laws is not permitted during the transitional phase. Exceptions to this are laws enacted by citizens in the direct legislative process.

---

[166] §61.4-9 Election of persons process

9.9.4.3 Election programme

Each party wing draws up an election programme at a programme party congress, which states how the party wing envisages the future work of the minister or senior worker. Party wings with similar ideas can form coalitions to develop a common election programme. Individuals can form a new party wing to be able to put forward their own programme. The working groups of the party wings send all their developed position papers as motions to the Programme Party Congress. All programmes must consist of programme items that are based on the organisation chart of the respective ministry. It is listed which department is to be expanded, dismantled, reorganised, abolished or newly established. All programme items must be accompanied by amounts and justifications for costs and revenues or benefits. All planned revenues and expenditures shall be listed and given a time period in which they will be incurred. Costs and revenues should be given for all programme items and for the programme as a whole, so that coalition negotiations can be conducted more easily in the committees after the pre-elections.

In each programme, information must be provided on how the area of responsibility is to be managed. To this end, specific details of work instructions to the responsible non-elected staff of a ministry must be provided. A programme may, if necessary, include proposals for reform. This should include concrete information on laws that are to be created, changed or abolished. A justification must be formulated as to why it is necessary to change the current state of affairs. For all new laws defined in the programme, the results of the long-term simulation from the Algoracle[167] must also be published in the programme.

9.9.4.4 Programme election campaign

All election programmes of the party wings and coalitions are discussed with the population during the election campaign so that citizens can match their opinions with programmes

---

167 Ministry of Digital Affairs - 15.3 Algoracle

and programme items.

The election campaign begins at the latest 4 weeks before the pre-election. By then, all programmes that are to participate in the pre-election must have been filmed and published. The Ministry of Media Affairs films and publishes the programmes on Government Television.

The election campaign for the most popular programme is run by the party of the affected ministry. Election campaign costs are financed by party donations. The party is obliged to distribute the donation amount equally among each programme submitted.

9.9.4.5 Pre-election

At the end of the election campaign, voters decide in the pre-election which election programmes and programme items they like best. When voting, up to 3 programmes can be ranked. The ranking indicates which election programme those entitled to vote like best, better and most. Programmes that are well liked get one star, those that are better liked get two stars and those that are best liked get three stars.

Up to 10 plus points can be awarded to all individual programme items. A popular programme item can receive one point or all 10 points. The programme items do not have to be included in the programmes that have been ranked. In addition, up to 5 minus points can be awarded to programme items that are not liked by voters.

The pre-election results in the 3 most popular programmes and the 10 most popular programme items. The 3 most popular programmes are the programmes with the most, second and third most stars. The 10 most popular programme items are the 10 programme items that received the highest number of plus points minus their minus points.

9.9.4.6 Programme committee[168]

After the pre-election, the most popular 3 programmes and 10 programme items will be combined on the programme committee. The event can be extended to up to 5 consecutive days. Government Television broadcasts the events in real time.[169] Programmes may or may not be combined. Programmes that have won the pre-election can be combined into one programme if the programme items complement each other and do not contradict each other. This can be three or two programmes. This makes it possible to offer voters three, two or one programme for the run-off election. Popular programme items must be integrated into the programme that suits them best. If several programmes fit, several programmes can also include the same programme items.

The distribution of stars, plus and minus points indicates the popularity of all programmes and programme items. The following committees are guided by this data. On the committees, coalition negotiations are conducted between the party wings and the citizens and as many programmes as possible are combined. Popular programme items are included in a suitable programme. Five factors play a special role in this process. The factors are firstly the number of votes in stars for a programme, secondly the number of votes in plus and minus points for a programme item, thirdly the time in which a programme item is to be implemented, fourthly the relationship between costs, benefits and revenues, and fifthly the results of the long-term simulation from the Algoracle[170] . Based on these five factors, the programme items are divided into compatible and incompatible programme items and distributed into up to three programmes. Programme items that are mutually exclusive are placed in different programmes. Only one programme remains if all programme items can be combined.

Text amendments may still be made with a majority of 85% of the participants involved in the committee. For each programme and for each programme item, its implementation

---

168 §95 Committees in the election of persons process
169 Ministry of Media Affairs - 7.2.3.2 Programme committee
170 Ministry of Digital Affairs - 15.3 Algoracle

costs and implementation period must be specified. The financing of individual programme items can be rejected in the budget vote. This risk is pointed out by the moderators when the previous year's budget has already been exceeded and it is necessary to include all costly programme items.

9.9.4.7 Candidates[171]

Candidates are allowed to report for each electoral programme put forward for the run-off election. All candidates must be members of the party in whose area of accountability they are standing. They need not belong to any party wing. All party members who wish to run for the policy office report on the candidates' committee profile in the Committee Directory. All such candidates are invited to join the committee.
Candidates may stand for all electoral programmes that they can reconcile with their conscience. If they stand for more than one or all three election programmes, they must credibly justify this and pass the examinations for all programmes.
The posts advertised for election are those of politicians, i.e. ministers, their deputies and senior officials in a ministry. Senior staff are policy posts in the ministry. They include, for example, moderators, head of the note issuing bank[172], judges[173] and intendants of the state broadcasting authorities. Other or less directly elected senior officials can be appointed by citizens at any time in a staff quorum.

9.9.4.8 Candidates' committee[174]

As soon as the programmes from the programme committee are available, the candidates' committee is convened. The candidates' committee usually consists of several committee meetings held on up to 5 consecutive days. The Government

---

171 §60,2-5 Eligibility
172 Ministry of Finance - 10.4 Note-issuing Banks
173 Ministry of Justice - 5.6.1 Judges
174 §60.1 Eligibility: BV Art.143, §61.1 Election of persons process, §95 Committees in election of persons process

Television produces the associated television show.[175]

On the individual committees, as in a casting show, the candidates' abilities are tested and ranked by votes of those entitled to vote. Each candidate is allowed to present themselves in the public casting, which is broadcast on state television. There is no jury, only the audience. The audience in the studio and on the screen can rate statements in real time. The discussion tools of the Solution Finder[176] are available for this purpose.

At the end of the candidates' committee, the 2 most popular candidates are determined to compete for a post and the implementation of a programme in the run-off election. The video clips in which the candidates explain their programme are available individually on the intranet as election information. If three programmes have emerged from the pre-election, up to six candidates can be nominated for the run-off election.

9.9.4.8.1 Round of introductions

At the beginning, each candidate has to express their motivation in up to 60 seconds. Each candidate must explain why the programme they are running for is the best and why they are the most qualified to implement it. Then, in up to 60 seconds, they should say which programme they are running for, what education and work experience they have had, how old they are and where they have lived so far. This is also possible in a pre-produced video. Candidates are allowed to support these statements with freely selectable media and instruments. This information is already communicated on the candidates' committee profile. All eligible voters select via their People's Computer whether a candidate will advance to the next round. Those who receive more than 50% approval move on to the next round.

---

175 Ministry of Media Affairs - 7.2.3.3 Candidates Committee

176 Ministry of Media Affairs - 7.2.3.5 Solution Finder (Legislation Committee)

9.9.4.8.2 Simulation games

Afterwards, the qualifications are tested in simulation games. All candidates compete against each other in several simulations. In games with the character of a game show, the candidates demonstrate their skills on stage. Everyday political situations are simulated and the audience can observe how the candidates work. In terms of the schedule, the situations are structured like in a simulation game for well-known parliaments such as "SIMEP"[177] . The scenarios are taken from the computer game "Policy Manager".[178]

During the simulation game, the voters have the opportunity to cast a vote for the deselection of each candidate. As soon as 50% of those entitled to vote have activated the "deselection" button on their People's Computer, the candidate is eliminated. In the first simulation game, the candidates have to act out crisis scenarios for the official area of responsibility in a representative democracy procedure, working together as well as possible to overcome the crisis as quickly and favourably as possible.

In the next simulation game, each candidate has to work individually in their virtually recreated future office and work through an everyday working day with tasks and work instructions for their workers. Suddenly, situations arise that require the candidate to decide whether and how active he should now become. In this simulation game, the candidate puts on a virtual reality suit, complete with Virtual Reality glasses, microphone and headphones. He moves around in the virtually recreated inland and can use all the means that would be available to him in his office. The crucial thing is that all candidates play through the same scenario at the same time, but cannot see how the other candidate does it; only the spectators can do that.

In the last simulation game, the election programme is run through in fast motion. Each candidate only stands for the programme for which he or she has applied. The maximum of three programmes are simulated one after the other. While one programme group of candidates plays the simulation, the

---

177http://www.simep.eu/
178Ministry of Digital Affairs - 15.5 Policy Manager

other programme groups have a break.

9.9.4.8.3 Final test

Finally, there are questions about policy expertise needed in the ministry. The schedule is similar to a quiz show. However, why questions are asked in which facts and ethical attitudes have to be explained. The viewers thus decide whether the answers are right or wrong as they see it. They can choose the last two most popular candidates from the remaining candidates one last time.

9.9.4.9 Candidate campaign

The successful candidates advertise their programmes during the election campaign and discuss with the population how they would take into account the defeated minority in office. All campaign events and committees for the election of persons are broadcast on Government Television. During the election campaign, candidates go on the trail of the programme. Places, citizens, companies and colleges related to the programme are visited. Each candidate completes internships in the respective places where the programme is supposed to have an impact and asks the colleagues there what they think of the programme, what would be good and what would be bad about it. Each candidate is supposed to keep a video diary and publish it in his or her profile in the Labour Directory. The Party Television makes a report out of it and broadcasts it before the run-off election week.

9.9.4.10 Run-off election

After the election campaign, the voters decide which programme should be executed by which candidate in office. Depending on whether several programmes have emerged from the pre-election, those entitled to vote choose one between two or three programmes, or reject or approve the one combined programme. When voting, all the programmes put forward for election are listed, and behind them their candidates. After each programme, a choice can be made between voting in favour and voting against. The vote for approval may only be cast once or not at all.

After this vote, those entitled to vote can choose between approval and rejection after each candidate. For each programme, including rejected ones, approval can be given only once or none for the two corresponding candidates. In addition to the profile picture, name, education level and profession, the test results from the committees are also listed. The candidate with the majority of votes of at least 65%, wins the run-off election and must implement the programme for which he or she contested.

If the necessary majority of 65% is not achieved for a programme, the pre-election must be repeated, in which only the three programmes with the most votes from the first pre-election compete against each other. Another run-off election follows.

If the necessary majority of 65% is not achieved for one candidate, the run-off election must be repeated, in which only the two candidates with the most votes in the first run-off election compete against each other. The majority of over 50% of the votes then applies.

9.9.4.11 Familiarisation

Successfully elected candidates are inducted into their office as politicians. To do this, they accompany the outgoing politician at work. Ministers simulate legislation in a trial run. If the previous politician had to resign immediately due to the quorum, the responsible Federal Moderator takes over the induction.

The familiarisation period applies to all persons who have never held the post before. It is 6 weeks and a maximum of 5 months if postgraduate studies are required. Politicians at national and international level must have a degree in the specialist department of their ministry before taking office. If there is no degree in the specialist department, postgraduate studies must be completed. Politicians attend a state college for 3 months and receive a short programme of study there. This includes an insight into the studies of the specialist department. Afterwards, 3 different internships are completed for 2 weeks in companies, authorities and associations of the remit in order to get to know the practice on which the politician will decide.

9.9.5 Three ways of election of persons

The election of persons can be direct, indirect or representative. The citizens decide which path to take by means of a veto quorum or participation quorum. The paths can also cross. At the beginning, citizens, politicians or councillors can ensure a new election. In the committees on the programme and candidates, either citizens or councillors can vote. For voting, those entitled to vote can be citizens, delegates or councillors.

9.9.5.1 Direct election of persons

In the direct election of persons, the citizens have met the deselection quorum. All party wings present their election programmes in the election campaign and put them to those entitled to vote in the pre-election. In the pre-election, citizens determine the 3 most popular programmes and the 10 most popular programme items. In the programme committee, popular programmes and programme items are combined or separated by the citizens. In the candidates' committee, the party wings present their candidates and the citizens select two candidates for each programme and put them forward for the run-off election. In the run-off election, the citizens choose a programme and the candidate who belongs to it.

9.9.5.2 Indirect election of persons[179]

In the indirect election of persons, the politician has resigned of his or her own accord. All party wings present their election programmes during the election campaign and put them to

---

179§106.4 Responsibility for government and control

the pre-election of those entitled to vote at the party council. In the pre-election, the delegates determine the 3 most popular programmes and the 10 most popular programme items. In the programme committee, popular programmes and programme items are combined or separated by the citizens. In the candidates' committee, the party wings present their candidates and the citizens select two candidates from each programme and put them up for the run-off election. In the run-off election, the delegates of the party council choose a programme and the candidate who belongs to it.

9.9.5.3 Representative election of persons

In the representative election of persons, a majority of councillors support the vote of no confidence in the politician. All party wings present their election programmes during the election campaign and submit them to those entitled to vote as deputy ministers for pre-election. In the pre-election, the deputy ministers determine the 3 most popular programmes and the 10 most popular programme items. In the programme committee, popular programmes and programme items are combined or separated by the deputy ministers. In the candidates' committee, the party wings present their candidates and the deputy ministers select two candidates from each programme and put them up for the run-off election. In the run-off election, the deputy ministers select a programme and its candidate.

Ministers may be elected by the deputy ministers. International ministers may be elected by outgoing ministers, deputy ministers and municipal ministers. Municipal ministers may be elected by the municipal delegates.

The representative election of persons for municipal ministers and politicians is conducted by the municipal party council as follows: In the third way of the election of persons in the municipality, all party wings represented in the municipality present their election programmes in the election campaign and present them to those delegates entitled to vote in the municipality for pre-election. In the pre-election, the delegates determine the 3 most popular programmes and the 10 most popular programme items. In the programme committee, popular programmes and programme items are combined or separated by the municipal party congress. In the candidates' committee, the party wings present their candidates and the municipal party congress selects two candidates from each programme and puts them up for the run-off election. In the run-off election, the delegates choose a programme and its candidate.

9.9.5.3.1 Chain of legitimacy

Should the citizens be so weary of voting that they want all elections of persons to be representative, they can form a legitimacy chain. Through the legitimacy chain, deputy ministers are elected by the municipal party council and meet in the council of ministers to elect national ministers. National ministers, in turn, meet together with their deputies as an international council to elect international ministers. A chain of legitimacy applies to one ministry at a time. New elections are held through the deselection quorum, for which citizens are entitled to vote.
If citizens want to regain their voting rights, they can cast their vote for the corresponding participation quorum.

9.10 Legislation[180]

The people decide in the constitution which provisions are to become laws. These are all basic provisions for citizens on the exercise of political rights, the limitations of constitutional rights, the rights and duties of persons, the group of persons liable to pay taxes, and the object and assessment of taxes. It also includes all basic provisions for citizens in the state service on the functions and performance of ministries, the obligations of municipalities to assist in the implementation and enforcement of legislative provisions, and the organisation and procedure of the authorities of all ministries.

180§75.1 Legislation: BV Art.164

9.10.1 Flexible use of the legislative process

When we speak of a law here, the legislative process exemplifies the process of creating the most diverse norms of the ladder of norms.[181] It is always a matter of drafting texts that provide humans with guidelines for action in state policy. Even if other norms of the ladder of norms are not actually subject to voting, citizens can demand that the legislative process be applied to other norms or state treaties. When "committee" is mentioned here, it exemplifies the processes that take place in committees and can be applied to any negotiation with many affected parties. The Ministry of Digital Affairs provides the necessary software free of charge and the hardware for a fee.[182]

9.10.2 Numbers as numerals in laws

As many norms as possible should contain numbers as numerals that can be entered in the course of a voting. Instead of only being able to indicate "approval" or "disapproval" and "deselection", a number can then also be entered by the voter. In the count, the average or median can then be included as a number in the norm. This makes it more likely that a new norm will be approved, because those who would reject the norm only because the numbers are wrong, but the text and purpose are good in themselves, can also approve the law and do not have to reject it.

9.10.3 Right of initiative[183]

The right of initiative allows ministers, deputy ministers, party members and citizens to introduce drafts or templates into the legislative process. The Federal Moderator's Office checks the validity of all initiatives that have come about. This involves checking whether the persons introducing the initiative have the right of initiative. All ministers can submit their initiatives

---

181 Ministry of Justice - 4.6 Ladder of norms
182 Ministry of Digital Affairs - 13 People's Innovation Company Intranet
183 §72 Right of initiative and petition: BV Art.160, 173, §73 Implementation of initiatives

as templates directly for voting. They can turn drafts into templates with their staff in the ministry or in the Council of Ministers. All deputy ministers can submit their drafts to the minister and turn their drafts into templates in the Council of Ministers. Party members can submit their drafts to the minister and turn their drafts into templates in the Party Council. The minister decides whether to put the submitted templates to a vote.

All citizens can open an initiative quorum with their initiative. As soon as 10% of those entitled to vote are in favour, a draft is turned into a template in a committee or a template is voted on directly.

Initiatives that ministers, deputy ministers and party members may introduce are laws, municipal laws, regulations, administrative instructions and service instructions. Citizens may also introduce constitutional articles as initiatives.

If several ministries are affected by an initiative, the ministers must agree on the distribution of responsibilities. If no agreement is possible, the responsibilities are distributed either in a committee or by the responsible Federal Moderator.

Before templates may be voted on, they must have been filmed and broadcast on state television.[184] Those entitled to vote are affected citizens, the people or peoples, depending on the specific scope of the initiative. Before the initiative can come into force, it must be supported by a majority of those entitled to vote in a ballot.

9.10.4 Counter-proposal

Counter-proposals are treated like initiatives with the following exceptions. Counter-proposals always arise when several mutually incompatible solutions to a policy problem are invented. They are admissible if the existing legislative initiative is not to be changed, but incompatible opposites must find a place in another text.

Counter-proposals can be introduced by ministers or deputy ministers if citizens have introduced an initiative. If ministers have introduced an initiative, citizens or deputy ministers may

184 Ministry of Media Affairs - 7.2.2 Filming of laws

introduce a counter-proposal.

Deputy ministers have the task of implementing the will of the citizens in their municipality. They can introduce Counter-proposals to apply to their municipality in all three ways. These counter-proposals are introduced as municipal law if more than 60% of the affected citizens of the municipality vote in favour of the counter-proposal. If a majority also votes in favour of the counter-proposal in another municipality or in the whole country, it becomes a municipal law or law there as well.

Depending on which legislative route is taken, there are different options for citizens.

Petitions may contain Counter-proposals, which must be marked as such. Ministers may take up or reject these counter-proposals. An initiative quorum may also include a counter-proposal. If 10% of those entitled to vote support this initiative quorum, the counter-proposal is introduced. The counter-template is put to the vote at the same time as the bill. If it is a Counter-draft, it is formulated into a Counter-template before voting in a Committee, a Council or in the Legislative Directory. Which procedure is to be used is always decided by the authors of a Counter-proposal or by the citizens with a veto quorum.

Citizens can upload their Counter-proposals to the committee's profile up to 7 days before the initial vote on a committee. They are included in the initial vote of the committee. Counter-draft proposals can be formulated on the committee or in the Legislative Directory for a template. Counter-drafts can also be created during a committee and are formulated directly into a template there.

Counter-proposals can also be introduced into the legislative processes of representative democracy. The formulation of a Counter-draft towards a Counter-template is done by the responsible Council and the voting on Counter-templates is done by the responsible Council if the citizens demand this by veto quorum or participation quorum.

9.10.5 Law-making provisions[185]

All norms of the ladder of norms are considered law-making provisions. The people enact the articles of the constitution. Ministers issue laws and regulations, judges issue court decisions, deputy ministers issue municipal laws and other elected politicians also issue statutes, administrative instructions or service instructions. Citizens are responsible for establishing habits.

Ministers can transfer all law-making provisions to their area of accountability if 60% of citizens demand it after a participation quorum. Ministers can also call a voting on the matter.

All Law-making provisions are profiled in the Legislative Directory during the making of law. All adopted Law-making provisions are given a profile in the Law Directory.[186] In the directories, the profiles are provided with links to the possible quorums. Citizens can intervene in the legislative process at any time through a veto quorum. They can replace elected politicians at any time through a deselection quorum. They can change or delete a law that has already been enacted by means of a repeal quorum. The same applies to enacted articles of the constitution through the revision quorum.

Laws are all norms that are written in law books. There is a code of laws for each ministry with guidelines for action for the respective ministry and the citizens. Above this is the constitution. It specifies how the state is to be constituted and is at the top of the ladder of norms. Laws may not violate its articles. Those who violate laws receive sentences for it, which can be found in the penal code.[187] The rules that citizens must observe among themselves are found in the Civil Code.[188]

All other norms can be treated procedurally in the same way as the political processes for laws, if the citizens demand it in the veto quorum. This reduces the number of procedures for citizens to a few familiar ones and keeps the dynamic

---

185§74 Form of enactments: BV Art.163, §75,2-7 Legislation: BV Art.51, §104,3,4,6 Government decisions

186Ministry of Justice - 4.7 Law Directory

187http://www.gesetze-im-internet.de/stgb/StGB.pdf

188http://www.gesetze-im-internet.de/bgb/BGB.pdf

media democracy comprehensible enough for all citizens to participate.

9.10.6 Digitised legislation

In the Law Directory[189] , a profile is created for each new enacted norm, i.e. from constitutional articles to service instructions for state employees. Constitutional articles and laws must first be voted on by the people before they are entered in the Law Directory. During the drafting phase, these norms are filed in the Legislative Directory, where citizens or politicians can create profiles for problems or proposed solutions. If lobbyists are involved in the creation of norms, this must be listed in the Lobby Directory and broadcast on state television. The voting behaviour of politicians from parties, councils and ministries is filed in each profile first in the Legislative Directory, later in the Law Directory and in the Labour Directory.

In this way, the entire process from creation to provision to abolition is presented and stored on the intranet. Citizens can easily participate in the legislative process as users of the intranet. Regardless of whether ministries or citizens work with this data or have a say in it, all participants have access at all times. In this way, the dynamic media democracy works transparently on the one hand and participatively on the other. Transparent means that every citizen can see who is currently working on which norms or which norms already exist. Participatory means that all users can create, comment on and rate profiles in the Legislative Directory right from the start. A new profile is worked on until it is ready for majority approval. However, new profiles only become norms when they are issued by the responsible minister and approved by a majority of those entitled to vote. Importantly, a standardised profile makes it easier to campaign for a new norm, while the network community discusses and rates the project throughout the development process.

Once the law is in force, citizens can see how often and in which court proceedings the law was applied. This is possible

---

189 Ministry of Justice - 4.7 Law Directory

via the Court Directory.[190]

9.10.6.1 Legislative Directory

In the Legislative Directory, profiles can be created for issues and proposed standards so that other users can comment and rate them. The profiles are created by citizens and politicians for each newly conceived norm. Politicians are obliged to do this in order to guarantee citizens their right to a veto quorum. If politicians face a problem, they can ask citizens for help by creating a new profile.

When citizens create the profiles, they can also export profiles of proposals to the Quorum Directory in order to open a new profile for an initiative quorum there with the data. Citizens can export issues to the Petition Directory to start a new petition with the data.

In the Legislative Directory, the working groups of all parties and lobbyists from the Lobby Directory are represented as groups.

9.10.6.1.1 Homepage

On the home page, there is a folder structure on the left, arranged according to the ministries, up to current legislative processes. In the middle is the standards pinboard, where at the top proposals for new standards can be posted by users as a profile. Below, these proposals can be discussed, reworded, linked to other norms or problems, and rated. On the right side is the Problem Pinboard, where problems can be posted by users as profiles at the top. Below, these problems can be discussed, rephrased, linked to other norms or problems and rated. When writing and connecting proposals, the user is supported by the functions of the modulator.[191]

---

190 Ministry of Justice - 5.5 Court Directory
191 Ministry of Digital Affairs - 14.5 Modulator

9.10.6.1.2 Folder structure

In the Legislative Directory, all profiles of current legislative processes are sorted by ministry in a folder structure. Clicking on them displays the profile of a draft or template for a new norm, which has a timeline in the upper half of the screen. The timeline shows where a proposal is in the process and how many votes it already has. This makes it clear whether only citizens or a party or even a ministry is already drafting the proposal for the law. As soon as a template has been approved by voting, the profile is transferred to the Law Directory. During the entire legislative process, it is possible to view the working papers of the ministries and parties and, as a user of a People's Computer, to write comments on them or to rate passages of text.

9.10.6.1.3 Proposal

In a profile for a new norm, one must enter the wording in a text field. Then you have to select which standard this proposal should become. For this purpose, there is a selection menu that contains all norms of the ladder of norms[192] . Now the proposal should be linked to only one or, if necessary, to several responsible ministries. The automatic keywording of the entered wording in the text field displays norms from the Law Directory that have similarities with the proposal. In addition, the user can search the Law Directory for similar norms. The proposal is automatically linked to the folder structure of the Law Directory in a future display, so that authors know where in the Law Directory the new norm should be listed later. Other users can add to these links later on the standards pinboard. However, the author of the proposal decides which link will be included in the profile of the proposal. Proposals can be drafts that have yet to be negotiated, or templates that are directly ready for voting. This decision is made by authors themselves, although those entitled to vote can request a negotiation in the committee through the veto quorum.

---

192 Ministry of Justice - 4.6 Ladder of norms

9.10.6.1.4 Problem

In the profile for a current unsolved problem, users must enter the wording in a text field. Then select which ministry is responsible for this problem. If possible, you should only name one ministry, but you can also select several. For this purpose, there is a selection menu in which all ministries that are to be responsible are marked with a tick.

The automatic keywording of the wording entered in the text field displays norms from the Law Directory that have similarities to the problem. Users can also search the Law Directory themselves for similar norms. The aim is to link the problem to the Law Directory so that it becomes clear which law needs to be amended or abolished, or where a new law needs to be inserted to remedy the problem. Other users can add to these links later on the problem pinboard. Authors of the problem decide which link should be included in the problem's profile.

9.10.6.2 Simulation in the Algoracle

The simulator Algoracle[193] is used to simulate the impact of laws. For this purpose, the mainframe computer of the Ministry of Digital Affairs records all existing norms and all recorded data of the citizens and companies within the country in order to virtually represent life in the inland today. Foreigner influences are simulated with as much statistical data as possible. Laws and deciders that have been formulated can now be entered into the simulator and all changes that can be attributed to them will be displayed. Everything is possible, from changes to the constitution or to the distribution of competences of municipalities to the national or international level and vice versa.

This simulator is similar to the computer game series "Anno". The graphic is the satellite image of the inland and a click on a town hall shows the politic situation of the town, for example tax revenues, expenditures, companies, birth rate, suicide rate, debt rate, savings and savings rate. The Ministry

---

193 Ministry of Digital Affairs - 15.3 Algoracle

of Digital Affairs is responsible for ensuring that all data is collected, processed and displayed as results on the intranet. This simulation programme is available to all users of the Legislative Directory. Use can be restricted for citizens to keep investigations or defence tactics secret. Certain functions can only be performed in the intranet café. Each new norm is automatically simulated before voting with a history of 2, 10, 50 and 100 years. The result is displayed as a link in the voting.

9.10.7 Controversial laws[194]

Contentious laws are discussed with the population when there are camps in the population that want the law at all costs, but also camps that want to avoid the law at all costs. Such a situation damages the cohesion of the population. Therefore, the citizens should be given the opportunity to come together in a committee.

Which laws are controversial becomes apparent when, in the course of reporting, many citizens debate a law and it receives many votes in the rating options on its profile in the Legislative Directory or Law Directory. The Ministry of Media Affairs then intensifies its coverage of this law and broadcasts at least two views of the different camps. Here, journalists are forbidden to take sides.[195] The views are presented in feature films, reportage or videos produced by the owners of a view and uploaded to the Media Directory .[196]

If citizens are bored by it, they will not cast their vote on the intranet or try to express their opinion via the comment function. But if citizens are interested in a law or a proposed law, whether they are in favour of it or against it, the importance for the population as a whole increases. Ultimately, the deciders are those who oppose the law and those who want to influence the wording of the law through a veto quorum or repeal quorum.

194 §75.4 Legislation
195 Ministry of Justice - 8.12.3 Biased reporting
196 Ministry of Media Affairs - 5.6 Media Directory

9.10.8 Urgent laws[197]

If there is imminent danger, laws can be declared urgent by responsible councils of ministers and immediately come into force for a limited period. The time limit ends at the latest with the next budget vote, in which all current urgent laws must be put to the vote.

Urgent laws can be declared controversial laws by citizens and thus be co-determined and voted on earlier by citizens. The veto quorum must remain active during the period and is triggered by as little as 20% of those entitled to vote. Only after urgent laws have achieved a majority in a voting, they can only be changed or abolished by the repeal quorum.

Laws declared urgent without a constitutional basis may only enter into force for a limited period after a vote of the people with a majority of 75%. The time limit ends after a constitutional committee if in the voting the amendment, deletion or addition of articles was accepted by a majority of 80% of the people.

9.10.9 Provisional laws[198]

All ministers have the right to make laws at any time. All laws are considered provisional until they have received over 60% approval in a voting. This voting can either be called directly by the responsible minister or at the end of a committee in which the law was negotiated, or at the latest during the next budget vote. In the annual budget vote, all laws enacted in the previous year are on a list per ministry for a legislative vote on which no vote has yet been held.

Provisional laws that are not in the best interests of the citizens are either negotiated within the year until the next budget vote over a veto quorum of 30% of those entitled to vote in a committee, and possibly amended or abolished. After laws have been endorsed in the budget vote, they can only be amended or abolished by a repeal quorum of 60% of those entitled to vote in a committee.

197§87,2j Mandatory referendums: BV Art.140, §76 Legislation in case of urgency: BV Art.165
198§75.3 Legislation

If ministers too often enact laws that are not in the interests of the people, their deselection quorum will increase. Whenever voting on a law, the responsible minister must always be listed next to the voting question and a tick can be put behind his or her name for "deselection".

All provisional laws come into force after voting, unless the minister specifies a probationary period, which may last at most until the upcoming budget vote.

9.10.9.1 Probationary period

Ministers can bring provisional laws into force for the duration of the probationary period before a vote. The probationary period can be used to test the effect of a law. From enactment to voting, these laws are in the probationary period. If regularisations prove ineffective or flawed during this time, the text of the law can be amended or deleted.

If the minister decides with the participants of a committee to enact the law itself without holding a vote after the committee, the same probationary period may also apply to laws from a committee.

If enacted laws are abolished or amended during the probationary period, any sentences that have become invalid as a result must be remitted and repaid. The amounts must be saved until the voting. Laws that result in imprisonment or state expenditure may not have a trial period. They shall be enacted only after the voting.

9.10.10 Lobbyists in the legislative process[199]

In a legislative process, it often happens that stakeholders from companies or associations want to influence legislation. This is possible, but must happen publicly, either in front of the cameras of state television or on the panel of a committee. Lobbyists can make appointments to attend a joint meeting. These meetings take place on a regular basis and allow all lobbyists to present their concerns at the same time, so that all

---

199 §65 Prohibition of instruction: BV Art.161

concerns are heard for the same amount of time, a discussion can be held between opposing interests and no one-sided over-influence occurs. Meetings with lobbyists must be specifically justified and lobbyists involved, their interest group and their concerns must be made public in advance. No monetary payments or gifts may be made by or to lobbyists. All meetings must be broadcast on state television.[200] Politicians and lobbyists may face imprisonment if they violate this rule.[201]

9.10.10.1 Lobbyists

Lobbyists are all representatives of companies, associations, clubs or other organisations who want to influence policy. They can submit their concerns through personal meetings, speeches via video, sound or text. No matter how the media video, image, sound or text are transmitted, they must in any case be digitised and published by the recipient on the intranet. Recipients are all state agencies. The presentation on the intranet is done via the Lobby Directory.

9.10.10.2 Lobby Directory

In the Lobby Directory, each lobby has a profile. All lobbyists working for a lobby organisation are listed here by name and linked to their profile in the Labour Directory. Anyone who claims to be a lobbyist in their profile in the Labour Directory and does not belong to a lobby group will have their own profile in a new lobby group in the Lobby Directory. The decisive factor for a lobby representation is how many persons from the Persons Directory and companies from the Labour Directory follow the profile of a lobby representation. In the case of foreigners and foreign companies, a valid address must be given at which the represented persons or companies can be reached.

The ad offers a search function on the homepage and a list of all recently active lobbyists. This list shows all contacts

---

200 Ministry of Media Affairs - 7.2.1.3 Lobby documentation
201 Ministry of Justice - 8.14.4 Non-transparent lobbying

between lobbyists and politicians. All broadcasters and recipients involved must be listed by name and linked to their profile from the Persons Directory or Labour Directory. The content of the lobby messages must be linked to at least one law or legislative project and one politician from a ministry.

In the Lobby Directory, all lobby messages are listed and sorted by date, ministry or lobby representation. Supporters and opponents of civil society, non-governmental organisations (NGOs) and companies being lobbied for or against can form groups.

Each entry must be published on state television. For this purpose, the lobbying agency films the entry. An entry must appear in at least one 30-second segment on the daily News Television[202] . The Ministry of Media Affairs is responsible for linking the broadcast content from the Media Directory to the entry in the list of lobby messages.

9.10.11 Three ways of legislation

Legislation can be carried out directly, indirectly or representatively. Which way to go is decided by the citizens through a veto quorum or participation quorum. These procedures always apply to legislation and can be used for other norms if citizens request this in a veto quorum. The other norms may be ordinances, municipal laws, statutes, administrative instructions or service instructions.

In principle, the normal state is indirect legislation and direct voting. In case of disinterest, representative legislation and indirect or representative voting can be chosen. In case of interest, direct legislation can be chosen.

9.10.11.1 Indirect legislation[203]

In the indirect legislative process, ministers can introduce an initiative, prepare the draft with their ministry for template. Deputy ministers and citizens can submit counter-proposals.

---

202 Ministry of Media - 8 News Television
203 §98.3 Ministers, §106.5 Responsibility for government and control

Counter-drafts are prepared with the ministry to form Counter-templates. Counter-templates are put to a vote together with the initiative.

The appropriate colleagues of the ministry meet in the council building with the initiators. The minister is represented on behalf of the ministry, as well as responsible politicians and staff members who are concerned with the initiative's subject area. Together they transform initiatives and counter-proposals into templates for voting. The meetings are broadcast in real time on state television. If several ministries are affected, they are entitled to vote. A Federal Moderator then takes the chair. In indirect legislation, national ministers are responsible for national laws and international treaties, international ministers for international laws, and deputy or municipal ministers for municipal laws. Direct legislation is mandatory for controversial laws and government decisions without a basis in the electoral programme.

A veto quorum can be used to switch to the direct or representative legislative process for this individual case. A participation quorum may be used to switch permanently to the direct or representative legislative process for that ministry. The minister is free to call in committees or councils for advice or to switch to the direct or representative procedure during the legislative process.

9.10.11.1.1 Interview

Ministers address surveys to citizens. The questions can be answered via a profile page for issues in the Legislative Directory, as part of an interactive broadcast on state television or in the form of a voting. If the question is very complicated, it can also be answered by a committee.

9.10.11.2 Indirect voting[204]

In the indirect voting procedure, delegates from the affected party vote simultaneously on templates and counter-templates that have had votes lent out by those entitled to vote. They publish their voting behaviour for borrowed votes in the party council and in slogans.

If those entitled to vote want to cast their vote themselves, they can do so and the borrowed vote is cancelled. This changes the voting procedure to the direct voting procedure. A veto quorum can be used to switch to the representative voting procedure for this individual case. Through a participation quorum, all future voting for the ministry can be done with the representative voting procedure.

9.10.11.3 Direct legislation[205]

In the direct legislative process, citizens can submit a citizens' initiative once the initiative quorum has been met. The draft is prepared in a committee for the template. Ministers and deputy ministers can submit counter-proposals. Counter-drafts are prepared on the Counter-template committee or reconciled with the initiative. In a reconciliation of drafts and counter-drafts, the demands of both initiatives can be taken into account and only one template is produced. Counter-templates are put to a vote together with the initiative.

The committee meets in public places with a panel, audience and spectators. The negotiation procedure corresponds to the show concept "Solution Finder"[206] and is broadcast in real time with citizen participation on Government Television. The panel will include the responsible ministers and guests appropriate to the topic. The audience consists of affected or interested citizens as far as possible. The location of the committee is chosen to match the topic.

People's Committees are responsible for national laws, Peoples Committees for international laws and treaties, Citizens

---

204 §100.4 Party Council
205 §104 2b,3,6 Government decisions
206 Ministry of Media Affairs - 7.2.3.5 Solution Finder (Legislation Committee)

Committees for municipal laws.

The committee is free to call in ministries or councils for advice or to switch to the indirect or representative procedure during the legislative process. A participation quorum may permanently switch to the indirect or representative legislative process for that ministry.

9.10.11.4 Direct voting[207]

In the direct voting procedure, citizens vote on templates and counter-templates simultaneously during an election week. Citizens who do not vote and have lent out their vote thus switch to the indirect voting procedure. A veto quorum can be used to switch to the representative voting procedure for this individual case. Through a participation quorum, all future voting for the ministry can be carried out with the representative voting procedure.

9.10.11.5 Demonstration

Citizens have the right of assembly. The registration and supervision of demonstrations is regulated and carried out by the Ministry of Security.[208] The Ministry of State Organisation takes on the task of issuing laws on which political assemblies are considered demonstrations and how they may proceed in order to be considered a lawful political means.

If citizens wish to revolt against a political condition, they may assemble, freely express their opinion and demonstrate peacefully at any time. If more than 100 persons gather for a demonstration, a participant in the demonstration must call the police so that they can secure the demonstration procession in road traffic. Demonstrations with more than 1000 expected participants must be registered with the local police station. If a demonstration is advertised publicly, the date must also be reported to the local police station. Demonstrations must not last longer than 24 hours if they are within a 10 kilometre

---

207 §104 2b,3,6 Government decisions
208 Ministry of Security - 4.9 Demonstrations

radius. This is to avoid blockades of entire neighbourhoods. Demonstrations for the purpose of industrial action in the Free Market Economy may only be blocked by affected companies. If a counter-demonstration has been registered for a demonstration, a People's Motor Vehicle will be ordered from the Ministry of Media Affairs. If the demonstrations want to block or fight each other, they will be separated. Participants of both demonstrations who are willing to talk can report to the People's Motor Vehicle staff. The People's Motor Vehicle will set up between the two demonstrations and set up tables and benches where participants from both demonstrations who are willing to talk should talk to each other. These moderated talks will last 15 minutes and follow a regular schedule.

Firstly, the two interlocutors greet each other. Secondly, the first person is allowed to talk for 3 minutes about why he is going to the demonstration and should describe his opinion, evidence, experiences and fears. Thirdly, the second person is allowed to talk for 3 minutes about why he is going to the counter-demonstration and should also describe his opinion, evidence, experiences and fears. Fourthly, both interlocutors now have 8 minutes to exchange ideas about solutions that they both have. As soon as solutions are found that both interlocutors would agree with, these proposed solutions should be reported to the People's Motor Vehicle staff.

After the demonstrations, a committee is held at the People's Motor Vehicle, which must be attended by the responsible municipal or national politicians from the affected ministries. There, all the proposals for solutions that have been collected are discussed.

Demonstrators who are willing to use violence have to report to the police so that they get an opportunity to fight. For this purpose, an area is cordoned off, the size of which depends on the number of participants of those who would like to fight. Those who enter this area know that they are putting their lives in danger and have to pay a participation fee to the Addictive drugs Health Insurance[209] to cover the health costs for wounded people.[210]

---

209 Ministry of Health - 5.12.3 Addictive drugs Health Insurance
210 Ministry of Security - 6.6.3 Brawl

9.10.11.6 Petition[211]

A petition can consist of praise, criticism or suggestions for improvement. These suggestions should have something to do with the work of one or more ministries or with state services that are necessary or unnecessary. In the same way, they can also be regulations for companies, business ideas or new innovative products.

It is possible to select individual responsible staff members in the individual organisational charts of the ministries to whom the petition is addressed. If citizens are unsure who is responsible, the Federal Moderator's Office must provide information within 3 working days.

Once all the necessary submissions have been made, the petition can be published. All petition publications must be reported on state television. A period of 2 weeks runs from the day of publication. Within this period, authors of a petition can advertise for support.

A petition consists of a real and virtual signature list. On a real signature list, citizens must state their name, date of birth and place of birth and submit their signature. These real lists have to be digitised in the town hall. All the citizens' details are automatically matched with their profile in the Persons Directory. There is an entry about this data retrieval in the access log. The support of this citizen is entered in the profile of the new norm in the Legislative Directory.

Via the People's Computer or in the intranet café, signatures are set virtually by the user agreeing to the petition. When a citizen has invented a new norm, he or she creates a profile for it in the Legislative Directory.

If a petition reaches 50% of the votes of the affected population, the petition must be discussed within 2 days in an interactive show of the Government Television with affected politicians and citizens and, if necessary, a solution must be found.

At the end of the 2 weeks, responsible ministries are obliged to examine the petition. A decision is made as to whether the suggestion should be taken up or rejected. The decision, including the reasons, is communicated to the authors within 6 months.

---

211 §34 Right of petition: KV Art.20

If ministries accept a proposal, they implement it and may adapt it. If parties take up a proposal, one or more party wings adopt it, turn it into a citizens' initiative and advertise it to mobilise majorities.

If ministers and parties announce their rejection and the petition has been used to advertise an initiative quorum, the initiative quorum can remain open until approval rises above 10%.

If a counter-draft to an initiative is introduced, a petition can be used to get 0.005% of those entitled to vote to support it within 2 weeks. This allows a counter-template submitted by citizens to take part in the voting on various templates of an initiative.[212]

9.10.11.6.1 Petition Directory

Citizens can start petitions by creating a new profile in the Petition Directory. To do this, they write at least one text with their request. Additions in the form of sound, image or video recordings can also be added. Users have the opportunity to make comments and ratings on the petition. Via this profile, other citizens can click on "Support petition" and confirm their automatically set personal data to add their virtual signature to the list. Supporters and opponents can exchange views in groups.

9.10.11.7 Citizens' initiative[213]

Citizens' initiative is a proposal for a new norm or government action. Citizen initiative includes proposals for new inter-municipal or international treaties, division of responsibilities between ministries, opening or closing of a ministry, other government decisions, and any norms on the ladder of norms. These are constitutional articles, laws, court decisions,

---

212§91 Procedure for initiative and counter-draft: BV Art.139b
213§89 Initiatives by citizens: KV Art.58, 59, §72,4 Right of initiative and petition, §73,4 Implementation of initiatives

ordinances, municipal laws, regulations, administrative instructions, service instructions or customs. Initiatives can be introduced as drafts or as templates. Drafts are negotiated in a committee, where they are transformed into a template. Templates are put directly to a vote of those entitled to vote. Citizens can open a new initiative quorum in the Quorum Directory by creating a profile for it. Through questions, instructions and keywords, a programme guides users through the professional formulation and submission of the initiative. All authors are listed in the new profile and can be contacted by the responsible state agencies for any queries. If there is any confusion about the responsibility of ministries or politicians, the Federal Moderator's Office is responsible for advising authors of an initiative.

Once the initiative has been submitted, it must be audited by the responsible ministry within 2 weeks. Responsible ministers can still implement the initiative before the quorum is triggered. If the initiative is rejected, authors can keep the initiative quorum active indefinitely.

9.10.11.7.1 Invalidity of citizens' initiatives[214]

If an initiative is declared invalid, it must be demonstrably unworkable or violate fundamental rights. The authors are notified of the results of the review with the justifications and legal regularisations affected. Then the authors are allowed to seek advice from the responsible party and remedy any deficiencies in order to update the initiative. All supporters who had cast their vote are asked via the People's Computer whether they wish to continue to support the initiative in this way. The changes will be marked in colour. Authors can also refuse to support the initiative and leave the initiative quorum active. If an invalid initiative quorum nevertheless reaches 10% of those entitled to vote, the responsible ministry must convene a committee and then schedule a vote, regardless of whether the initiative is a draft or a template.

---

214 §90 Invalid initiatives: KV Art.59

9.10.11.7.2 Election campaign for citizens' initiatives

After the examination, the authors can use the party's campaign opportunities for 14 days. The authors decide on the distribution of days and funds. This includes services from the ministries of media and digital. The initiative must be filmed according to the authors' wishes and broadcast on state television in voting with the authors. The film rights are held by the authors, and in the case of commercialisation, 10% of the profits must be paid to the Ministry of Finance[215] . The Ministry of Digital Affairs provides automated web pages that are fed from the data of the initiative quorum profile and can be modified and evaluated by the authors. This website can also be accessed via the digital in the initiative quorum profile in the Quorum Directory.

9.10.11.7.3 Counter-proposals for citizens' initiatives[216]

Counter-proposals can be submitted as soon as the quorum is running. Counter-proposals can participate in the committee as a draft or can also be introduced as a template in the voting. Politicians can submit counter-proposals directly. Citizens can only submit a counter-proposal if 0.005% of those entitled to vote support a petition for this initiative within 2 weeks. Those entitled to vote can vote in favour of several templates. If the voting results do not differ by at least 5%, a run-off vote must be held between the two leading templates.

9.10.11.8 Committee procedure for laws

The committee procedure can be held in different forms. In order to develop laws or other norms together with all those affected, the following form is used. In committees, citizens discuss and formulate a ministry's draft laws after a majority vote on the veto quorum or participation quorum.

---

215 Ministry of Finance - 11.7 Government Account
216 §91 Procedure for initiative and counter-draft: BV Art.139b

9.10.11.8.1 Virtual preparation

Each committee is given a profile in the Committee Directory. The Legislative Directory already has at least one profile of an issue or proposal related to the committee's project. Matching profiles from the Legislative Directory are linked to the newly created Committee Directory profile in the previous week. In this way, a discussion on the best proposed solutions and formulations for one or more norms can be written, commented on and rated by the users. Part of the virtual preparation is that problems and proposals for norms are filmed one week before the start of the committee and broadcast on state television.

9.10.11.8.1.1 Norms pinboard

For each problem that 30% of the users agree with, suitable proposed solutions for norms are published by the users on the norms pinboard, commented on, modified if necessary and rated. Similar profiles on the norms pinboard can be displayed by users by creating a link via the modulator[217] to the matching profile. In addition, an algorithm automatically suggests similar proposals to users who are currently viewing the norms pinboard, so that users are the controllers and determine an actual similarity, not a computer programme. If users see a similarity, they can press the "Link" button. Once 20% of the users have done this, the two profiles are linked and unified into one profile. The proposed solutions are usually still changed or discarded by the virtual discussion. The texts produced in the profile for a proposal for norms are later used in the committee. The proposals that are selected are those that have not been rejected by more than 40% of the users in the rating and in which at least 50% of the users have been involved in the rating.

The day before the committee, this preliminary vote is closed. The 10 most popular proposed solutions are presented at the committee. The authors are invited to the committee. A committee always deals with only one problem or

---

217 Ministry of Digital Affairs - 14.5 Modulator

requirement to be addressed by one or more norms. In the digital preparation, all attitudes of the ministry, the party and the citizens are summarised. Statements by members of the ministries or parties are colour-coded. Groupings are formed as to which formulations are similar to each other and which formulations are opposed to each other.

9.10.11.8.2 Real preparation

Proposals or problems can also be submitted at events. They are immediately digitised and matched with all profiles from the Legislative Directory. Similarities are marked and similar profiles are automatically combined. Initially, all new real proposals and problems submitted are listed, as well as the virtual proposals with the most positive ratings. Opposing popular proposals are discussed in People's Motor Vehicle in public places and broadcast in Government Television. In discussion groups, attempts are made to make the proposals capable of gaining majority support. Preference is given to proposals that have different and mutually exclusive approaches to the same topic. First, two groups are formed to clarify the opposing formulations. The moderator asks the audience to express agreeing or disagreeing opinions at different stages.
In the first phase, only those who are in favour of the proposal currently under discussion should speak. They should find a common wording that all those in favour of the proposal are satisfied with. This is how it goes with all the proposals one after the other. Once this phase of "consolidation" is completed, the phase of "discussion" begins.

9.10.11.8.2.1 Discussion

Now, supporters and opponents of a proposal are to publicly exchange their arguments. All arguments are collected and listed. The participants involved vote on the relevance of arguments. In this way, the arguments are ranked. For example, the list of pro-arguments may be shorter than the list of con-arguments, but twice as many participants may have voted for the fewer pro-arguments. This would give a majority for the pro-arguments.

9.10.11.8.2.2 Finding a compromise

In the final phase of "finding a compromise", arguments have to be weighed against each other or solutions and formulations found that satisfy both sides equally.
The proposals for solutions developed flow back into the virtual preparation as a proposal and into the initial vote at the committee.

9.10.11.8.3 Procedure

The procedure of a committee corresponds to the show concept Solution Finder[218] , unless those entitled to vote or responsible ministers provide for a different concept. The necessary adjustments are listed in this chapter.

9.10.11.8.3.1 Report

The 3-minute reports incorporate the results from the problem pinboard and the discussion phase. The results are filmed using examples from everyday life, at best edited together from past news programmes on private and state television and online video platforms.

9.10.11.8.3.2 Initial vote

The 10 most popular proposals from the norms pinboard and the compromise phase are included in the initial vote.

218Ministry of Media Affairs - 7.2.3.5 Solution Finder (Legislation Committee)

9.10.11.8.3.3 Moderators

Three moderators moderate the committee. The panel moderator is sent from the Federal Moderator's Office, the voting moderator from the Ministry of Digital Affairs and the audience moderator comes from the Ministry of Media Affairs. The responsible minister is not a moderator himself in order to be able to participate in the discussion in a concentrated manner. Moderators of committees, like all other politicians, have a deselection quorum.

9.10.11.8.3.4 Panelists

Responsible politicians and rapporteurs always sit on the panel. Rapporteurs can be responsible employees of the state, a company, an association, a non-governmental organisation, a scientific institute, a college, affected persons or representatives of the party wings selected by the party.

9.10.11.8.3.5 Video contributions

Guests from the audience may report for a speech and speak live in front of the camera. Guests who do not dare to speak live can record their video statement in the TV box next to the People's Motor Vehicle. Audience members can record a video statement with their People's Computer. For this purpose, the front camera is activated and a specially written text can be read from a teleprompter. All recorded video statements are immediately uploaded to the Committee Directory profile and can be rated by all audience members. All guests in the audience can view and rate the video statements on set-up touch screens just like on the People's Computer. To vote, you have to hold your voting card in front of the camera on the screen to scan the QR code. This prevents multiple votes. The screens are set up in a ring around the People's Motor Vehicle so that they do not interfere with the recording of the panel discussion, but the text is still clearly audible. If necessary, 10 headphones hang from cables on one screen.

The most popular video statements are broadcast on the stage screen and on state television during the So-called "opinion break". As soon as a video statement has the mark of 100 000 views and good ratings, an "opinion pause" is shown to the voting moderator. The ongoing discussion on the panel pauses and the video statements are played as the opinion of the people.

The video statements may already be uploaded as soon as the committee's profile page is available on the intranet. This way, positive ratings for a video statement can already be collected during the preparation time.

9.10.11.8.3.6 Solution letter

The developed solution letter is used as a basis for the next committee in another city or as a template for voting.

9.10.11.9 Representative legislation[219]

In the representative legislative process, councillors can introduce initiatives and so can citizens once the initiative quorum has been met. The draft is prepared in a council for the template. Citizens can introduce Counter-proposals through an initiative quorum. For each initiative and counter-proposal, 30% of the councillors in the councils must agree to a negotiation.

The council meets in the council building with the initiators and selected expert rapporteurs concerning the initiative's subject area. Together they transform initiatives and counter-proposals into templates. Counter-drafts are prepared in the council into counter-templates or reconciled with the initiative. In a reconciliation of drafts and counter-drafts, the demands of both initiatives can be taken into account and only one template is put to a vote. All Council meetings are broadcast simultaneously on the Government Television and stored for public access on the intranet. If several ministries are affected, those responsible for the councils of all the ministries involved are entitled to vote.

---

219 §104.2c,4 Government decisions

In representative legislation, the Council of Ministers is responsible for national laws, the International Council for international laws and international treaties, and the municipal party council for municipal laws. Direct legislation is mandatory for controversial laws and government decisions without a basis in the electoral programme.

A veto quorum can be used to switch to the direct or indirect legislative process for this individual case. A participation quorum can be used to switch permanently to the direct or indirect legislative process for that ministry. The council is free to call in committees or politicians for advice or to switch to the direct or indirect procedure during the legislative process.

9.10.11.10 Representative voting[220]

In the representative voting procedure, the councillors vote on templates and counter-templates simultaneously. The votes are held in public in the Council building with a show of hands by the Council members.

Through a veto quorum, it is possible to switch to the direct and indirect voting procedure for this individual case. Through a participation quorum, all future voting for the ministry can be done with the direct and indirect voting procedure.

9.11 Constitutional amendments[221]

The Ministry of State Organisation is responsible for organising all policy procedures for constitutional change. The Federal Moderators moderate the constitutional committees and the Minister of State Organisation convenes constitutional referendums.

Only the people have the right to make changes to the constitution. The constitution can be revised in its entirety, only individual constitutional articles, only individual paragraphs or only individual numerals.

The Constitution may only be amended by direct legislation

---

220 §104.2c Government decisions
221 §253 Constitutional amendments: BV Art. 192

through direct democratic participation of the people. The committee and voting procedures shall apply subject to the following adjustments. Borrowed votes to delegates of the Party Council do not count for constitutional referendums. All nationals have equal voting rights and voting is compulsory for constitutional referendums. Compulsory voting does not apply to citizens living abroad.

Depending on whether only individual articles are reworded, abolished or added, or whether the entire constitution is to be revised, constitutional amendments take a maximum of 5 years or only a few weeks.

The Constitution shall remain in force until amended. The amendments shall take effect as soon as all the votes cast have been counted and the final official result is announced by the Minister of State Organisation. At that time, the Constitution in its old form shall cease to be in force and the Constitution in its new form shall come into force.

9.11.1 Constitutional initiative[222]

Initiatives can be submitted to amend the constitution. Those who wish to revise all or part of the Constitution open a new profile in the Legislative Directory and select the relevant initiative. Citizens can also submit their initiative to the Town Hall Office of the Ministry of State Organisation, which will publish it in the Legislative Directory. Authors can share writing privileges for their initiative only with themselves, with a closed group or with all users. The level of detail in the profile indicates whether the initiative is a suggestion, a draft or a template. Suggestions are characterised by the fact that they can be vaguely formulated and unstructured. Drafts already resemble a template, but are still open to reformulation. Drafts may already have been reviewed by the parties for state organisation and foreign affairs to ensure that they do not contradict the constitution and international law. Templates must have been reviewed by the parties and cannot be changed once they have been published.

As soon as authors publish their initiative, they automatically

---

222§257,1,2 Constitutional initiative: BV Art. 139

open a revision quorum. After publication, authors can release writing rights for all users to turn suggestions or drafts into templates. Once the revision quorum has been triggered, the formulation into a template takes place at a constitutional committee.

9.11.1.1 Review[223]

Prior to publication, an author of an initiative may seek advice from the foreign affairs and state organisation parties. The advice includes a review of the initiative and suggestions for improvement if it violates international law or the constitution. The Party for Foreign Affairs examines whether the initiative violates international law. The party for state organisation checks whether the initiative violates the constitution.

Once the revision quorum has been met, a constitutional initiative is reviewed by the Foreign Office[224] and the Guardians of the Constitution. The Guardians of the Constitution check whether it violates other articles of the Constitution. If a constitutional initiative violates the rest of the constitution, all other affected articles are also adjusted in the Constitutional Committee. This means that a template or Counter-template cannot be put to a direct vote, but must first be negotiated in a committee.

After the revision quorum has been fulfilled, the Foreign Office checks whether a constitutional initiative violates international law or international treaties. It informs those entitled to vote about this on state television. If the constitutional initiative receives a majority in the constitutional referendum, the repeal quorum for the affected international agreements is automatically fulfilled. The repeal quorum is followed by a committee and voting, as well as renegotiation or exit from the relevant international law treaty. The Ministry of Foreign Affairs is responsible for renegotiation or exit.[225]

---

223 §257,4,6,7 Constitutional Initiative
224 Ministry of Foreign Affairs - 4.6 Foreign Office
225 Ministry of Foreign Affairs - 4.6 Foreign Office, 4.7 Embassies

9.11.1.2 Counter-initiative[226]

Once an initiative has been published, counter-drafts or counter-templates can be submitted. The same procedure is used for this and a separate revision quorum is opened. However, the profile must indicate which initiative is affected and whether it is a Counter-draft or a Counter-template. Counter-drafts can be tabled up to the start of the constitutional committee. If the revision quorum of the counter-draft is not triggered by then, it can continue as an independent initiative or be closed by the author. Counter-templates may be tabled until the day before the election week for the constitutional referendum. The proviso remains that the revision quorum for the counter-template has been triggered and that the counter-template has already been filmed so that it can be shown on state television at the beginning of the election week.

9.11.1.3 Counter-template by the Constitutional Committee[227]

If a template is not formulated in a legally secure manner, violates one or more articles of the constitution or international law, the constitutional committee drafts a counter-template. The special thing about a counter-template by a constitutional committee is that the counter-template tries to preserve the content of the original initiative as best as possible. This means that the committee identifies the affected legal provisions from the constitution or international law and adapts the initiative to them.

9.11.2 Constitutional Committee

The Constitutional Committee is a special form of committee. The individual events are structured in the same way as a committee, but the duration is usually longer and therefore more events are held per article. Negotiators also discuss laws that are directly or indirectly affected by the amendment of

226§257.3 Constitutional initiative
227§257.5 Constitutional initiative: BV Art. 139

a constitutional article. The responsible politicians and party wing leaders are always guests on the panel.

If the Constitutional Committee drafts several articles in templates, the constitutional referendum shall not take place until all articles have been drafted in templates. If necessary, it may be necessary to newly revise templates that have already been drafted. For example, the constitutional committee for a total revision may drag on for several years. In a voting quorum, the people can divide the constitutional referendum into individual votes in order to have individual chapters become law more quickly. The constitutional referendum procedures also apply accordingly to all individual votes.

If more than 20% of the population voted against an article in the constitutional referendum, all affected articles are newly discussed in the Constitutional Committee. Citizens who voted against are invited to attend the relevant meetings of the Constitutional Committee. They are invited via their People's Computer to come to the panel during the Constitutional Committee. This invitation is secret and citizens are not obliged to accept it. The secrecy of the ballot applies, but with this exception it should be possible to hear the dissenting voices so that a majority consensus can be found.

9.11.3 Partial revision[228]

A partial revision means the amendment of individual articles of the constitution. If only one article is affected, 2% of the people must have participated in the corresponding revision quorum. For an article to be affected, it is irrelevant whether a new article is inserted or an existing article is amended. If several articles are affected, 10% of the people fulfil the revision quorum. For example, if a chapter requires the amendment of 2 or 12 articles in order to anchor the content of the constitutional initiative in the constitution accordingly, 10% of those entitled to vote must be involved in the revision quorum.

Initiatives that are introduced as a template and whose revision quorum is met are put directly to a constitutional referendum.

228§255 Partial revision: BV Art. 194, KV Art.128

All other initiatives or rejections of a constitutional article in the Law Directory are negotiated in constitutional committees and drafted into a template. A constitutional committee is held for individual articles as well as for articles that are related in substance. Several appointments may be made for this if the content is too extensive. Thematically separate articles are negotiated one after the other in separate committees. When formulating the templates, the unity of the constitution must be observed in the partial revision. Individual innovations must not contradict the rest of the constitution.

9.11.4 Total revision[229]

A total revision means the amendment of the entire constitution. It is carried out as soon as a total of 25% of the people have participated in a revision quorum. For example, if 0.5% of the quorum for the revision of 50 articles has been met, a total revision is carried out. For example, if an initiative to amend the entire constitution is submitted as a template, 25% of those entitled to vote must contribute their vote to the revision quorum in order to trigger a total revision.
Should a constitutional initiative in the form of a template for a new constitution have met the revision quorum of 25%, the people vote directly on this template. In all other cases, several constitutional committees are held in succession to prepare templates. In the first committee, an inventory is made of which articles are disputed and which are not. In further committees, all disputed articles are discussed one after the other and, if necessary, reworded or deleted. If there are constitutional initiatives in the form of suggestions, drafts, counter-drafts, templates or counter-templates of individual articles, they are included in the negotiations. In a final committee, the order of all articles is revised and the chapters and titles are finalised. Before the new constitution can be voted on, the template must have been filmed and broadcast by the Government Television .[230]
In the constitutional referendum of a total revision, up to two

---

229§254 Total revision: BV Art. 193
230Ministry of Media Affairs - 7.2.2 Filming of laws

different constitutional bills may be put to the vote. If there is only one draft constitution, there may be one template and two counter-templates for each individual article. Those entitled to vote have the option of voting on each article separately or voting in favour of individual chapters altogether. Articles that have not received the necessary majority of 80% are newly negotiated in constitutional committees. The total revision is only completed when the entire constitution receives the necessary majority. If the necessary majority is not achieved in the third ballot, the total revision is deemed to have failed. The old constitution then continues to apply.

To ensure that every generation gives its consent at least once to the constitution under which it lives, a constitutional referendum is held at least every 50 years. If 25% of the people then oppose the constitution in force, a total revision is carried out.

9.11.5 Constitutional referendum[231]

In the constitutional referendum, the citizens of the people have the opportunity to approve and reject templates and counter-templates. Either the digital ballot paper can include only one article or several, up to the entire constitution, depending on what the templates and counter-templates refer to. Those entitled to vote can reject individual paragraphs of each article and change the numeral in the text as they see fit. As soon as the templates and counter-templates refer to several articles, those entitled to vote will be able to reject each article individually or bundled together as an entire chapter. Those who have no objections at all, but fully agree with the template or counter-template, need only put a cross by "agree". All crosses for paragraphs, articles or chapters, as well as the change of numerals in texts, are considered as rejections. Voting for constitutional amendments, is video-monitored before and after entering the polling booth. The entire counting process of all votes is also video monitored and broadcast in real time on state television to prevent electoral fraud.

---

231 §258,1,2 Constitutional referendum, §259 Entry into force: BV Art. 195, KV Art.133

Votes on the constitution are also counted by hand. All counts are filmed, as is every step of the way until the results are published on state television. The entrance to the polling booth is filmed and the persons entering the polling booth are counted.

As soon as the revised constitution meets with at least 80% approval among the people in the final vote, it is deemed to have been adopted. If new norms, especially laws, become necessary as a result of the new constitution, legislative processes must be initiated immediately by the responsible ministries.

9.11.5.1 Compulsory voting in constitutional referendums[232]

Voting is compulsory in constitutional referendums and when the people have decided to hold several votes on individual chapters in a total revision. Domestic citizens living inland are obliged to cast their vote at a voting computer in any town hall in the country during the election week. Citizens are free to participate in the revision quorum or attend the constitutional committees. Those who violate the obligation to vote in constitutional referendums must serve one community service per article.[233] Voting rights in constitutional referendums cannot be lent out to parties, nor can they be given to councils.

10 Subsidiarity[234]

The principle of subsidiarity generally states that the individual is responsible for his or her actions and problem solving. The next largest group of humans helps when the individual cannot. For everything that would not be possible alone, the community is the reserve for each individual. Subsidiarity is derived from the Latin word subsidium, which means help or reserve. Family, circles of friends, clubs, companies, municipalities, nations and international unifications are considered interpersonal forms of organisation.

Subsidiarity is considered a principle in the state so that the

232 §258.3 Constitutional referendum
233 Ministry of Justice - 8.14.1 Violation of electoral duty
234 §52 Subsidiarity: BV Art.5a

individual can live in self-determination and all support each other in doing so. One for all and all for one should be the maxim for the direct democratic state. Therefore, dynamic media democracy extends the idea of subsidiarity and opens up to the individual the election between the responsibility of different political levels for solving problems that affect many humans.

The political level that can most effectively bring about a political solution should be responsible for it. As soon as one level is overburdened, other levels are obliged to be responsible. This change of responsibility is subject to the subsidiarity vote and can be adapted for a politician's remit, subject area or individual case.

The citizens themselves decide in whose responsibility state tasks are fulfilled most effectively and satisfactorily for the citizens. This means, for example, that it may be better for the consumption of resources if they are distributed locally, for example through Municipal Utilities Companies.

10.1 Subsidiarity principle[235]

Through the principle of subsidiarity, responsibilities are distributed in such a way that the body best suited for the solution is also responsible for it. What is the best solution is decided by the citizens together with politicians. Citizens can choose whether a law or state service should apply uniformly or vary from region to region. Municipal laws exist for this purpose. If a law is to apply in several countries, the Ministry of Foreign Affairs must negotiate a treaty with all the governments of the affected countries and have it voted on by all the peoples affected. If a ministry is to have effect in several countries, a subsidiarity vote must speak for it and the country must be in an international union in the middle ring with the inland.

The principle of subsidiarity leads to federalism. In the course of globalisation, federalism is the instrument to solve global problems internationally and local problems municipal.

235§132 Declaration of general applicability and obligation to participate: BV Art.48a

Only the state's monopoly on the use of force may only be governed centrally, so that war between federal member states can be ruled out. The state's monopoly on the use of force consists of the ministries of security and justice, which cannot be administered municipally but can be administered internationally. In all other policy remits, citizens can decide whether ministries are run municipal, national or international. In order to make the gradation even finer, it is also possible to have individual sub-areas within the ministries administered on a municipal, national or international basis. For all government decisions, citizens can demand by quorum that this individual case be decided at municipal, national or international level. For this purpose, the procedures for election and legislation are similar, but not the same, for the municipal, national and international levels. Citizens then do not have to learn different ways of working. What is different is the scope of those entitled to vote, the name of ministerial posts and the composition of councils.

The subsidiarity vote is the instrument of dynamic media democracy by which citizens can express their experience of successful task accomplishment by politicians. As soon as a sufficient number of citizens support the subsidiarity quorum or politicians demand it, a subsidiarity vote is held by the Ministry of State Organisation.

Areas of responsibility can be declared generally binding if the constitution or the people so provide. According to the constitution, these are the execution of sentences and measures, degrees at schools and colleges, cultural institutions of supra-regional importance, waste management, sewage treatment, environmental pollution control, long-distance transport, cutting-edge medicine and special clinics, institutions for the integration and care of the disabled, basic research and priority research. Other areas can be added through a subsidiarity vote.

10.2 Subsidiarity motion

For responsibility to be shifted between political levels, there must be something like a call for help. Citizens and politicians can send out this cry for help. They should describe how a political level is failing to provide a policy solution or service. Citizens open a subsidiarity quorum in the Quorum Directory with the subsidiarity motion, after which a subsidiarity vote takes place.

The subsidiarity quorum can be opened for ministries or for a single government decision by a citizen. Whether an area is administered by the lower or upper level, a subsidiarity quorum can be run to shift responsibility to another level. As soon as 30% of those entitled to vote are in favour of shifting responsibility, a subsidiarity vote is called.

Ministers at all levels can submit subsidiarity requests directly to the Federal Moderator's Office. This is followed by an examination of how the political level is failing, where and why. If an improvement is expected at another level, a subsidiarity vote is convened.

For example, the nationals of a city decide to own and administer the Municipal Utilities Company themselves. The citizens of a municipality submit this proposal to their deputy minister of the Ministry of Infrastructure. If he does not want to submit the subsidiarity proposal to the Ministry of State Organisation, the citizens can open a subsidiarity quorum.

10.3 Subsidiarity vote[236]

The political processes can be municipal, national or international. The level at which a policy solution is most sensibly implemented is decided by the affected citizens in a subsidiarity vote.

If individual municipalities do not want to have a ministry administered centrally by the nation, they can administer it themselves after a successful subsidiarity vote in their municipality. If several nations want to jointly administer a ministry of their countries, they can abolish the nationally administered ministries in their countries after a successful subsidiarity vote and an international ministry takes over the administration. If the people want to administer a ministry nationally, they can do so after a successful subsidiarity vote. Subsidiarity votes take place 2 weeks before the annual budget

236§50.3 Nation, §129.1 Autonomy of municipalities: BV Art.47

vote. Once a quorum has been reached, no decisions may be taken that have not been voted on by a majority of the affected citizens. The subsidiarity vote may be brought forward at the request of the responsible ministers.

After a subsidiarity vote, individual or several ministries can be internationally, nationally or municipally responsible. The ministries of security and justice cannot be responsible on a municipal level. International cooperation between national or individual municipal ministries is carried out through the Ministry of Foreign Affairs.

Subsidiarity votes are evaluated in more detail because the majority ratios of those entitled to vote at the different levels play a decisive role. Depending on which levels are affected, the majorities of yes and no votes are considered separately. The separation is made either on the basis of the municipality or the possibly new alliance of municipalities or the entire nation or several participating nations.

A subsidiarity vote can shift responsibilities, both for the rule case and for an individual case. The rule case is the permanent administration of a ministry at one level. The individual case is the exceptional responsibility of a ministry at one level for a government decision and its consequences at another level. Citizens and ministers are entitled to this shift. Ministers at all levels can immediately apply for subsidiarity. Citizens must first meet a quorum. The subsidiarity quorum must be fulfilled for the rule case and the veto quorum or repeal quorum must be fulfilled for the individual case. If the subsidiarity motion is approved by the Ministry of State Organisation or if the relevant quorum is met, the subsidiarity vote takes place. If the individual case consists of a counter-template, attention is paid to the distribution of the majority ratios of those entitled to vote at the levels affected when counting the votes.

10.3.1 Majority ratios in the rule case

In the case of the transfer of responsibility in the rule case, i.e. of an entire ministry, the following majority ratios apply, which lead to the creation or degradation of a ministerial post. If 75% of the citizens in the municipality or in the alliance of municipalities agree and less than 50% of the people as a whole are against the shift of responsibilities, the municipality gets the responsibility. If 95% of the citizens of the municipality vote in favour, no more than 90% of the people may be against it.

If the municipality has the responsibility and more than 60% of the citizens of the municipality or the people vote in favour, the nation is given the responsibility. If more than 90% of the people vote in favour, no more than 95% of the citizens in the municipality may vote against.

In an International Union, if more than 75% of the citizens of all participating member states agree and less than 30% in any single people of a member state oppose the shift of responsibility, the international ministry is given responsibility. If the ministry is administered internationally and more than 60% of the people of a nation vote in favour, the nation is again given responsibility in that country.

10.3.2 Responsibilities and majority ratios in individual cases

In the case of transfer of responsibility in an individual case, it is sufficient to fulfil the veto quorum together with the counter-template and a majority of 65% or more of the citizens affected, the municipality, the nation or the International Union. The ministers of the other two levels to whom responsibility is to be transferred in this individual case are responsible for the Counter-template.

In the case of national government, if a municipal law is to replace a national or international law, the deputy minister is responsible for this.

If a municipal law is to be replaced by a national law in the case of municipal government, the national minister is responsible. If a municipal law or a national law is to be replaced by an international law in the case of international government, the international minister is responsible.

If, in the case of national government, an international law is to replace a national law or municipal law, the foreign ministers of the affected countries are responsible and coordinate their action with the affected ministers.

In any legislative process, citizens of the municipalities or the nation can limit the scope of the law to municipalities or extend it to the nation by veto quorum. When a law is created, it should be possible to change the scope of application by veto quorum from the first proposal in the Law Directory[237] . In order to be able to inform oneself sufficiently, all minutes or working papers are available in written form or as a video. Any text inserted by a citizen or minister can be attributed to the person.[238]

Once a law is in place, citizens of the municipalities or the nation can subsequently extend or limit its scope by means of a repeal quorum. This requires an 80% majority at the municipal level and a 75% majority at the national level. All changes to the scope of laws must be negotiated in a People's Committee. It is necessary to justify why the validity of the law at the respective level is more beneficial to the general welfare of the affected citizens or the people.

The research institute[239] of the Ministry of State Organisation is investigating whether there are regularities according to which certain responsibilities work best for certain topics or departments. Politicians, private individuals and companies from the Social Market Economy, Planned Economy and Barter Economy are asked to send experience reports and completed questionnaires to the researchers. The intranet will be used for this purpose.

10.4 Subsidiarity Agency[240]

The Subsidiarity Agency is responsible for the smooth running of the distribution of responsibilities and the definition of the scope of application of laws. If there is any uncertainty as to whether the municipal, national or international level should be responsible, the Subsidiarity Agency is the appropriate contact.

A municipality can approach the highest level of government

---

237 Ministry of Justice - 4.7 Law Directory
238 Ministry of Digital Affairs - 14.5 Modulator, 15.5 Policy Manager
239 Ministry of Education - 11.7.2 State research institutes
240 §46.2 State

responsible for it directly if it sees problems with the distribution of responsibilities. The top level of government then contacts all those responsible and organises a contact meeting via video telephony. It is discussed how the problem can be solved. If the two levels cannot agree, or if the affected citizens demand it by a 50% majority, a committee is convened. If all participants involved agree, the top level presides and decides who can best solve the problem. The lower level has the right of appeal and can negotiate exceptions as long as the constitution is not challenged.

If any of the participants realise that a ministry involved is not able to solve a problem, they contact the Subsidiarity Agency. It is a nationwide body of the Ministry of State Organisation that can redistribute responsibilities. These redistributions can be put to a vote by quorum or negotiated in a committee.

11 Federalism

Federalism means establishing the political structures, processes and contents at the municipal, national or international level. As tasks and requirements change over time, citizens and politicians can recognise when one political level can satisfactorily handle a policy task or when another level would be better suited. Political reforms in particular can be tested well at the municipal level so that they can be applied nationally or internationally if they are successful. In order to be able to establish world peace, the state's monopoly on the use of force must be at the national level and, in the course of the communitarisation of states, be conducted at the international level until a new larger nation has emerged. The international level becomes obsolete as soon as the last federal state joins the united states of the world. An international level will then only be reintroduced upon the discovery of extraterrestrial intelligent life.

11.1 Definitions in federalism[241]

The political processes in the dynamic media democracy can be set in motion by ministers or citizens. Ministries and citizens are organised federally. In order to make a federal distinction here in the names of the political processes, a different prefix is used for committees and voting. For the national level, the prefix "people" is used. For the municipal level, the prefix "citizens" is used, and for the international level, the prefix "peoples" is used. The people represent all citizens of the entire nation. Citizens represents all affected citizens in a municipality or all those citizens who are affected by a policy. Peoples represents all the citizens of the affected countries. Ministers and politicians are preceded by the level for which they are responsible. Thus, there are international ministers, national ministers and municipal ministers, as well as, for example, municipal, national and international judges, as directly elected politicians. The procedural law remains the same for all elections of persons for ministers and politicians as well as for legislative processes. Exceptions apply only in the area of those entitled to vote.

Affected citizens can be citizens of a municipality, a nation, an International Union or citizens who are all affected by a local or factual circumstance.

Provided that the procedures function in the same way at all levels, the terms citizens, ministers, politicians, committees and voting are used without prefixes or adjectives.

Responsibilities are competences of several ministries, a ministry or areas within a ministry. Areas within a ministry may only be spun off to other levels if this means that it remains clear to the voter which minister is responsible for the activities of the ministry and its agencies. Politicians who violate their competences can be held accountable by the affected citizens through the deselection quorum.

---

241 §145 Federal Committees

11.2 Political levels[242]

The political structure is determined by the municipal, national and international levels. On these three political stages, the ministries, political parties and citizens play the decisive roles. All levels support each other in the fulfilment of their tasks, show consideration for each other and provide mutual assistance, office and legal aid. If disputes arise over the distribution of responsibilities, the Subsidiarity Agency intervenes and ensures negotiation and mediation. If necessary, a committee can be convened by the Minister of State Organisation or affected citizens after a veto quorum to resolve the matter.

If responsibilities are to be shifted between levels, a subsidiarity motion must first be submitted by responsible ministers or citizens, clarifying which responsibilities are to be shifted between which levels. If citizens submit this motion, a subsidiarity quorum is automatically opened. In the subsidiarity vote, it is decided whether and how responsibilities are to be shifted between which levels.

As soon as several ministries are involved in a decision affecting several levels, Federal Moderators moderate the procedures between nation and municipalities and the Ministry of Foreign Affairs[243] moderates the procedures between nations and municipalities of several nations. Moderation refers to the procedures for cooperation between ministries and the committees for negotiating treaties.

The three levels work together heterarchically and support each other. The municipalities receive instructions through national laws unless corresponding ministries become municipal self-governing after a subsidiarity vote or opposing municipal laws are enacted. Nations receive instructions through international laws if the peoples of the member states of an International Union vote in favour in a subsidiarity vote or vote in favour in a peoples' vote after an international legislative process.

242§126 Principles of federalism: BV Art.44, §138 Federal relations between several ministries; BV Art.172
243Ministry of Foreign Affairs - 4.7 Embassies

11.2.1 Constitutional order[244]

In principle, all levels must abide by the constitutional order. The municipal and national levels must observe the constitution of that country. The international level observes the constitutions of all member states. The national level ensures compliance with the constitution in the municipalities. The national ministries ensure compliance with the requirements of their representations in the municipalities. The people of a country ensure compliance with the constitution through the levels by means of direct democratic quorums, committees and voting, and the Constitutional Court.

The Minister of State Organisation intervenes when constitutional order is threatened or disturbed and, if necessary, arranges for an investigation by the Company Auditing Agency and the Surveillance Television or a People's Committee.

Ministries abroad prevent a violation of the constitutional order in their member states by exiting from shared responsibilities in the affected international ministry. The responsibility can only be shifted back to the relevant international ministry after a newly subsidiarity vote.

11.2.2 Primacy of law between the levels[245]

The law, which is set by the constitution, is supreme. Any law at the international, national and municipal levels must not contradict the constitution of the country. The constitution determines the constitutionality of a nation. National law, which is set by the people, protects the unity of the people and prevails over international and municipal law, which would endanger the unity of the people.

In order to protect minorities and to adapt to local conditions, municipalities may enact municipal laws that may conflict with international and national law, but not with the constitution. For the communitarisation of humanity into one people, the international level only sets such law that does not contradict

---

244 §131 Constitutional order: BV Art.52
245 §133 Precedence of and compliance with national law: BV Art.49

the applicable law of the member states. In doing so, every International Union at the international level pursues the goal of establishing legal equality between the member states. In this way, laws are to be formulated uniformly as soon as all participating peoples are prepared to do so by a majority in a voting.

The subsidiarity vote is there to obtain the consent of affected citizens as to whether or not law should be set at another level. Exceptions can apply to individual laws without forcing the responsibility of an entire ministry to be shifted to another level. International ministers and foreign ministers can introduce Counter-drafts or Counter-templates for the international level, deputy ministers and municipal ministers can do so for the municipal level. Those entitled to vote decide at which level the Counter-template should become law.

11.2.3 Implementation of the law[246]

Responsible for the implementation of the right are those political levels that have been chosen by the citizens. On the one hand, this allocation of responsibilities can be done through the constitution, on the other hand through a subsidiarity vote.

The implementation of the law takes place in the municipalities. Even if law has been set internationally or nationally, municipalities must implement it. In voting with their municipal deputies, ministers can set targets for when and how international or national law is to be implemented. As a general rule, whoever sets the law must bear the follow-up costs. Therefore, the national or international government sets up programmes to implement its law in the municipalities and pay for the implementation.

In order to be able to take appropriate account of municipal specificities and cultural minorities, the international or national minister coordinates with his or her deputies in the municipality. This is to enable a different implementation in the municipalities, through which a nationally comparable state service is available.

246§134 Implementation of the law: BV Art.46

Opposing municipal law may also be set in municipalities. Municipal law may be established through municipal laws, cultural protection areas, economic zones or ministries administered municipally. It must not conflict with the constitution.

11.2.4 Staff cooperation between levels in a ministry[247]

The cooperation between the employees of a ministry at different levels is heterarchical. Hierarchically above all employees, ministers and other elected politicians of a ministry are the citizens for whom the ministry is responsible. Accordingly, the international level is responsible for most citizens, the national level for fewer citizens and the municipal level for the fewest citizens. For the protection of minorities, however, municipalities have the possibility to enact exceptions through municipal laws. To protect the constitution, the nation must exclude the international level or force the municipal level to adhere to national constitutional law.

11.3 Responsibilities in federalism[248]

Responsibilities can be flexibly shifted between the political levels in federalism. The election of persons and legislation cannot be the same at every level and needs the following adjustments at the international, national and municipal levels.

11.3.1 National policy

The national minister is responsible when many, but not necessarily all, citizens are affected throughout the country. All deputy ministers make up the Council of Ministers. National ministers are directly elected by the people. If citizens of the people have lent out their vote, party members or party

---

247 §137,1-3,8 Interaction of national and municipal staff of ministries, §136 Relations between nations, nation and municipalities: BV Art.186
248 §144 Federal legislation, §140 Federal election of persons

wing leaders cast the vote by proxy. If the citizens of the people decide to cast their votes through a participation quorum, the Council of Ministers elects the national minister.

11.3.1.1 National election of persons[249]

In the first way, direct election, the election programmes are negotiated in a People's Committee and put up for pre-election. Candidates are determined in a People's Committee before the run-off election.
In the second way, the indirect election, the delegates of the national party council vote in the pre-election and run-off election. The citizens of the people can continue to cast their vote as in the first way, thereby automatically cancelling the vote of their delegate.
In the third way, the representative election, the Council of Ministers takes over the formulation and combination of the election programmes as well as the selection of the candidates.

11.3.1.2 National legislation

Draft laws or bills can be submitted directly by the national minister or, after a successful initiative quorum, by any citizen of the country. In the first legislative route, national ministers are responsible. They turn drafts into templates with their ministry. In the second path, the People's Committee takes over these negotiations and text formulation, and in the third path, the Council of Ministers. If there are counter-drafts, they are transformed into templates in the same way after the draft laws and put to the vote at the same time. If several ministries are affected by a law, the Federal Moderator's Office moderates this legislative process. The venues for the negotiation of the legislative text take place in the first and third ways of the legislature in the council building of the capital city. People's Committees are held throughout the country.

249§140,2,4 Federal election of persons

11.4 Global policy[250]

The international level is represented by the Ministry of Foreign Affairs or communitarised international ministries in international Unions or organisations. Only an International Union is considered a democratic political level. Only in such democratic procedures may competences be shifted to the government of a ministry. As soon as competences are transferred, it must be ensured that citizens continue to have at least the same direct democratic influence on government action as before.

The affected peoples vote in a subsidiarity vote on whether they agree to communitarisation of a ministry from the outer to the middle ring. In the outer ring, the international council consists of the national ministers and their deputies from the municipalities. In the middle ring, the international minister replaces the national ministers who leave office.

International laws and treaties are voted on individually by the affected peoples. However, when the peoples have obtained the representative form of governance through a participation quorum, the international council takes over the control and voting of government decisions.

The international level is above the national level after successful voting. International law then breaks national law and international ministries replace national ministries. The international or national and municipal levels still have the possibility to distribute responsibilities according to the principle of subsidiarity.

Once all ministries are communitarised, all peoples of this confederation give themselves a constitution, creating a new federal state with a national level that now governs more humans and a larger land area.

11.4.1 International Minister

The International Minister is responsible when many but not necessarily all citizens of all member states of the International Union are affected. He only gains this responsibility when a

---

250§143 International Government

subsidiarity vote has moved the government of this ministry to the international level. He retains responsibility and becomes the new national minister when states merge to form a new federal state for which he is responsible.

International ministers are directly elected by all affected peoples. If citizens of these peoples have lent out their vote, party members or party wing leaders cast the vote by proxy. If one or more peoples decide to cast their votes through a participation quorum, the International Council elects the international minister.

11.4.2 International Union[251]

Federal responsibility for ministries or laws can be at the international level if the affected peoples vote in favour. The procedure for transferring responsibilities of entire ministries accompanies the Ministry of Foreign Affairs in the International Union.[252]

In the outer ring, ministries of the member states reach agreements and can adopt joint laws with the same wording. The Ministry of Foreign Affairs moderates these legislative processes, as the Ministry of State Organisation does with national legislation, as soon as several ministries are involved in a government decision. At the international level, the same ministries of the member states work together. If several ministries are affected by an international policy decision, even more ministries are involved in the procedure. These procedures also apply to decisions of the United Nations[253] and to intergovernmental treaties.

In the middle ring, communitarised ministries of the member states are governed by international ministers directly elected by the peoples. Here, too, the foreign ministries of the affected member states take over the moderation and replace the tasks of the Ministry of State Organisation in this confederation in the procedures for the election of persons and legislation.

In the inner ring, all ministries are communitarised and the

---

251 §134 Implementation of the law: BV Art.46
252 Ministry of Foreign Affairs - 5.8 International Union
253 https://www.un.org/en/

peoples become a new nation as soon as they give themselves a common constitution. All formerly international ministries become national ministries. The Ministry of Foreign Affairs of this new federal state drives communitarisation with more neighbouring countries. Once religions have lost their divisive effect, the federal states of the continents can communitarise until there is only one federal state on earth.

The venues for the international election of persons and legislation are in the various member states. The public broadcast of the events is taken over by the state media institutions of the member states and simultaneously translated into the national language. Ambassadors and representatives of the Ministry of Foreign Affairs do the moderation, which at the national level is done by the Federal Moderators.

11.4.2.1 International election of persons[254]

The way to the middle level of an International Union is through the international election of persons.

In the first way, direct election, the election programmes are negotiated in a peoples committee and put up for pre-election. Candidates are determined in a peoples committee before the run-off election.

In the second way, the indirect election, the delegates of the international party council vote in the pre-election and run-off election. The citizens of all peoples can continue to cast their vote as in the first way, thereby automatically cancelling the vote of their delegate.

In the third way, the representative election, the international council takes over the formulation and combination of the election programmes as well as the selection of the candidates. Members of the international council are all deputy ministers from the municipalities. All Council members have equal voting rights and decide by a majority of at least 65% of the members.

254§140,3,4 Federal election of persons

11.4.2.2 International legislation[255]

International laws are laws that apply in all countries that declare themselves to be so. The wording of international laws is the same in all member states. The legislative process is the same as the national process. The citizens of all participating countries are entitled to vote.

Draft or proposed legislation may be tabled by the international minister or national ministers and, after a successful initiative quorum, by any citizen of the member states. Counter-drafts or counter-templates can be introduced by the deputy ministers, international or national ministers and citizens by initiative quorum. There are only national ministers in the outer ring and only one international minister in the middle ring.

11.4.2.2.1 Three paths of international legislation

The three ways of legislation also remain at the international level. If there are counter-drafts, they are transformed into templates together with the draft laws in the same way and put to the vote at the same time.

In indirect legislation, the national ministers are responsible in the outer ring and the international minister in the middle ring. They turn drafts into templates with their ministry. In the outer ring, the results of negotiations from the national ministries of the member states must be brought together in an international council consisting only of the national ministers. Unanimity of all Council members applies.

In the case of direct legislation, the citizens of all member states are responsible. The Peoples Committee takes over the negotiations for the formulation of the text from draft to template. The Peoples Committee applies equally in the outer and middle ring.

In representative legislation, the international council is responsible for developing templates from drafts. The international council has different compositions in the outer and middle rings. In the outer ring, the national ministers

---

255§144,2,3 Federal legislation

and their deputies from all the municipalities of the member states are members of the Council. In the middle ring it is the international minister and his deputies, as the national ministers no longer exist in the middle ring. All Council members have equal voting rights and decide by a majority of at least 65% of the members.

11.4.2.2.2 Responsibilities in case of different communitarisation

Member States may be in the outer ring of an International Union and enact common international laws or conclude treaties to unify the law. National ministers are responsible for these agreements. Member States may be in the middle ring of an international union and create joint ministries to oversee legislative processes and provide services. International ministers are responsible for these ministries.

The peoples committee or the international council meets in individual cases in international legislative processes if there is no international ministry in this departmental area. The same applies if several ministries are affected in an individual case, but not all ministries affected are administered internationally. The Ministry of Foreign Affairs moderates these procedures and the affected peoples must vote on them.

11.4.2.2.3 Voting

International laws may only be imported into countries where at least 75% of the people have voted in favour. Voting can be done either directly by those entitled to vote themselves, indirectly through party members and party wing leaders who have been lent out the vote, or representatively when the international council votes after a triggered participation quorum. Voting on international laws takes place either immediately after drafting or as part of the annual budget vote.

11.4.3 Financing of international ministries[256]

The funding of international ministries must be voted on once a year or in a multi-year financial framework in a budget vote with the affected peoples. If a people so decides, their national council of ministers or the international council can also vote on how much tax money should be allocated to the international ministry in the coming budget year. The costs are distributed equally per capita among all member states.

11.5 Municipal policy[257]

Municipalities can form their own municipal policy, which can be determined to a greater or lesser extent by the citizens of the nations, nation or municipality. The extent to which citizens of a municipality want to administer themselves is decided by them through municipal laws and subsidiarity votes.

Autonomy is guaranteed by the national and international levels as far as the constitution provides. Municipal autonomy is promoted through the municipal election of deputy ministers and their participation in government and law-making. Deputy ministers ensure that international or national policies are adapted to municipal circumstances. In the event of contradictions, municipal laws can clarify or extend international or national laws.

11.5.1 Municipality[258]

A municipality can be formed by at least 5,000 citizens living together in the same place. A municipality can therefore be the size of a small town or a large city and can consist of several municipalities. Each municipality has a town hall with a plenary chamber and an office for each ministry. Municipalities can exercise sovereign rights, but not in the policy areas of the

---

256§156 Principles for the allocation of tax funds: BV Art. 43a
257§129 Autonomy of the municipalities: BV Art.47
258§51 Municipalities: BV Art.3, §127 Population and territory of municipalities: BV Art.53

ministries of security and justice. A prerequisite for the self-government of ministries at the municipal level is a subsidiarity vote supported by a majority.

Municipalities exist by being founded, growing, shrinking and unifying. The municipalities do this on their own and let the affected citizens vote on it. The nation guarantees the municipalities their existence and the territory on which they are located. If the territory of the municipalities is to be changed, the people must negotiate and vote on this in a committee. If municipalities merely move territorial boundaries between each other, citizens of the municipalities must vote on the negotiated treaty. A veto quorum allows citizens to be involved in the contract negotiations.

11.5.2 Municipal level[259]

By default, municipalities are administered entirely by national ministries, i.e. by 18 ministers in the capital cities and their deputies in their town hall offices. The deputy minister is responsible if many but not necessarily all citizens of his municipality are affected.

The international or national ministers are no longer responsible for the ministry after the subsidiarity vote. The responsibility of the respective ministry for the affected municipality then lies only at the municipal level. Municipal ministers, conversely, no longer have responsibility at the national or international level. The citizens of the municipality lose their voting rights in the affected ministry for decisions at national or international level.

The ministries of security and justice are responsible for enforcing international or national law, but they must also respect and enforce municipal law. When a municipality administers itself, the national or international law of the affected ministry no longer applies in the municipality. Instead, the law of the municipally governed ministry applies. The authorities for security and justice observe and enforce the different legal situation.

259§134 Implementation of the law: BV Art.46, §128 Municipal self-determination

11.5.3 Municipal government[260]

The citizens themselves decide in a subsidiarity vote whether they want to be administered municipally, nationally or internationally and in which of the 18 ministries. Each municipality can administer all ministries itself if a majority in the subsidiarity vote is in favour. The ministries of security and justice and the drafting of a municipal constitution are excluded from municipal self-government.

The municipal minister forms the municipal government for his ministry. Government action corresponds to the procedures described above about governments. Exceptions are necessary for the election of persons and legislation. Municipal government decisions are not made by the council of ministers in the representative procedure, but by the municipal party council. The condition for this is that at least 90% of the citizens of the municipality have lent out their votes for the ministry in question to delegates. Delegates to the party council are local representatives from the responsible party. They can be party members who have had their votes lent out by citizens, or party wing leaders whose party wing has had votes lent out by citizens.

In the plenary hall of the town hall, the party councils of municipally administered ministries meet one after the other. If several municipal administered ministries are involved in a project, these ministries meet together. At these meetings of the municipal party council, the responsible minister comes with selected staff, according to the agenda. The procedure or new proposals of the municipal government are negotiated and voted on with the delegates of the affected party or parties in a public meeting.

11.5.3.1 Municipal election of persons[261]

The municipal election of persons elects deputy or municipal ministers. The deputy minister becomes a municipal minister if a majority of citizens vote in favour in a subsidiarity vote. A

260§141 Municipal government
261§140,1,4 Federal election of persons

new election is held only after a deselection quorum has been met. The election of persons process is adapted to municipal conditions as follows.

In direct elections, the election programmes are negotiated in a citizens' committee and put up for pre-election. Candidates are determined in a citizens' committee before the run-off election.

In the indirect election, the delegates of the municipal party council vote in the pre-election and run-off election. The citizens of the municipality can still cast their vote directly, thereby automatically cancelling the vote of their delegate.

In the representative election, the municipal party council takes over the formulation and combination of the election programmes and the selection of the candidates. For this, 90% of the citizens of that municipality must have lent out their votes to delegates to form a municipal party council.

11.5.3.2 Municipal legislation[262]

In the national or international legislative process, the deputy minister is responsible if a counter-template is introduced from the municipality or a majority of the affected citizens of the municipality demand a municipal law through a veto or repeal quorum.

The municipal minister is responsible for indirect legislation. The presiding municipal minister is responsible if several municipalities have formed an alliance. A citizens' committee is responsible for direct legislation. Representative legislation is handled by the municipal party council. The venues are either the local fairground or marketplace for a citizens' committee, the office of the municipal minister in the town hall or the largest meeting hall in the town hall for the municipal party council.

262§144,1,3 Federal legislation

11.5.4 Municipal laws[263]

Counter-templates can be introduced to laws that do not suit the circumstances of a locality. They can be introduced by the deputy ministers or the citizens of the municipality by means of an initiative quorum. If a counter-template is adopted in the voting by a majority of the citizens of the affected municipality, it is considered a municipal law. If a municipality wishes to enact municipal laws on its own, the deputy minister negotiates the proposal in the Council of Ministers. The template developed is put to a vote of the citizens of the municipality.

In the case of municipal self-government by the municipal ministers, only municipal laws are enacted for the affected ministry. However, the Council of Ministers is then no longer responsible, but the regular municipal legislative process applies.

Municipal laws have a repeal quorum and are listed in the Law Directory[264] , whether they were created by an international, national or municipal government. The nation respects municipal laws by applying them through the agencies of security and justice.

11.5.5 Financing of the municipalities[265]

The ministries provide the necessary funds to finance municipal services. Municipalities can set up their own businesses to finance themselves from their profits or to offer cost-covering services. Municipalities receive their own allocations as part of the budget vote, which citizens can determine directly.

The population of a municipality determines how much tax money that municipality is entitled to. The amount to be distributed is measured per capita, i.e. according to the number of citizens living in the municipality.

Municipalities whose ministries are administered nationally receive their funds from the budget of the national ministry. Ministries that are administered municipally receive their

263§142 Municipal laws: BV Art.51
264Ministry of Justice - 4.7 Law Directory
265§156 Principles for the allocation of tax funds: BV Art. 43a

funds per municipally administered ministry. The funds come from tax revenues generated in the municipality and are not earmarked as compulsory contributions for national or international services.

The distribution of funds for the coming year is also done through the budget vote in the case of ministries administered municipally. Citizens of a municipality can distribute their paid taxes there to municipal administered ministries of that municipality. For all tax revenues that are not distributed by the taxpayers themselves, the distribution is per capita. Exceptions are permitted if local circumstances so require and the people agree to the additional expenditure in the budget vote.

11.5.6 Cooperation between municipalities[266]

Municipalities may enter into treaties with each other and create joint institutions to provide state services more in the interest of the citizens. The treaties must be concluded using the same procedure as laws, must not conflict with the constitution and must contain substantive information on implementation.

An intermediate level is created when several self-governing municipalities form an alliance. They can administer ministries inter-municipally, enact municipal laws and create councils of ministers. The councils of ministers then consist of all participating municipal ministers and can be convened or dismissed after a successful participation quorum.

11.5.7 Cultural protection areas for the protection of minorities[267]

Cultural protection areas are zones with exceptions or supplements for laws and other social norms[268] , except for constitutional articles. Discrimination is permitted in cultural

266§139 Treaties between municipalities: BV Art.48
267§37 Cultural protection areas, §130,1,3,4 Cultural protection areas and economic zones: BV Art.50
268Ministry of Justice - 4.6 Ladder of norms

protection areas and may apply within the area. All special rules are noted on the town entrance sign and can be accessed online. There are signs for these similar to those used in road traffic. They are uniform throughout the country, but their inscriptions are usually unique.

In order to call a vote on the cultural protection area, an initiative quorum of 75% of those entitled to vote must be met. Only those citizens of that municipality are entitled to vote on the cultural protection area. In the voting, the citizens of a municipality can enact special rules for their municipality with a majority of 90% and from then on it is considered a cultural protection area. The turnout for this voting must not be less than 60%. All other decisions that follow in the course of time must be voted on with majorities of 80% or more by all citizens of the city who are entitled to vote.

For example, there could be a cultural protection area where all residents live in harems or all residents must have a certain appearance, wear special clothes and so on. Persons who do not meet the designated requirements are not allowed to stay in the cultural protection area. Exceptions apply to guests of residents or transients.

Municipalities can only declare themselves cultural protection areas if they can demarcate a contiguous living area. So in big cities, there can be no neighbourhoods as cultural protection areas that are not clearly separable from the rest of the city.

The Ministry of Integration is responsible for further legislation.[269]

11.5.8 Panel regulars' table

At the panel regulars' table, policy projects that affect one or more levels can be discussed. These events must be convened as soon as a subsidiarity quorum rises above 10%. The citizen moderator of the Ministry of State Organisation invites members of the affected party or parties for the policy project in the city. These meetings are to be held in a local catering establishment with a stage. The citizen moderator sits on the stage with the responsible state employees and the party

269 Ministry of Integration - 6.3 Cultural protection area

members sit in the audience, separated by party wings with 2 persons per table. Citizens of the municipality also take seats at these tables. So this becomes a panel discussion with a regulars' table atmosphere about a policy issue in the city. The panel discussions have to be announced to the state television in advance and are broadcast by the Local Television[270] . Because all citizens can never participate, the discussion is permanently available to all citizens on the intranet. At panel discussions, no decisions are made, but opinions and their majorities are sought, which have to do with the distribution of responsibilities between the political levels. The citizen moderator has the right to convene a committee with all affected citizens at any time. Citizens of the municipality also have this right by veto quorum.

12 State security

State security is considered to be at risk when persons in the state service do not comply with applicable law. Measures are taken below to prevent, detect and punish this. Persons outside the state service can also endanger state security. The Ministry of Security is responsible for these persons. In order for the state apparatus to deal with such a threat, a state of exception or state of emergency may be declared.

12.1 Corruption and crime in the state system[271]

The payment and receipt of money, goods or services for bribery to a state employee is a criminal offence.[272] Money, goods or services for the purpose of bribery are hereinafter considered as bribes. State employees must immediately refuse bribes and, if this is not possible, immediately file a complaint with the police or the public prosecutor's office. Anyone who pays a bribe is only exempt from punishment if the payment is reported immediately to a domestic police station. If a bribe is

270 Ministry of Media - 9 Local Television
271 §66 Prohibition of corruption §70 Supervision: BV Art.169, §71 Review of effectiveness: BV Art.170
272 Ministry of Justice - 8.1.2 Bribery, 8.14.3 Bribery of state employees

paid to the police, the report can also be filed with the public prosecutor's office. The complaint can also be filed on the intranet on the profile page in the Labour Directory of the state employees by placing a tick next to the field "Corrupt". A text field will open immediately where the date, time, place, amount of money, goods or services and the course of events are to be entered. The entries are displayed in the profile and immediately to the user of the profile. Other users can confirm this entry and also describe their experiences. Each entry is forwarded to the superiors, the police and the Ministry of Justice and collected. As soon as three bribery allegations are received from different persons, the state employees are reported by the public prosecutor's office. If it is a politician whose superior is the people, a committee of enquiry is convened.

The Ministry of State Organisation ensures the cooperation of all ministries to prevent, detect and punish corruption and crime in the state service.

The Company Auditing Agency audits state institutions.[273] The legal requirements of the Social Market Economy apply. The audit is conducted annually, but is covert one year and announced the next. Surveillance Television camera crews are allowed to be present during the unannounced visits .[274]

Citizens are involved in laws. If a law is more in the interest of a company or individual than in the interest of the citizens, the citizens are allowed to reject laws or to discuss and vote in a committee. This possibility exists at any time for every law via the repeal quorum and for every ongoing legislative process via the veto quorum. If effectiveness remains insufficient, citizens can remove politicians from office via the deselection quorum. Through the empowerment quorum, citizens can take overall control of a ministry.

The state TV channel Surveillance Television, together with free media and press representatives, carries out unannounced controls in all state institutions. The investigations may also be conducted undercover. Attempts to bribe as a covert investigation are permissible if they are filmed undercover.

---

273 Ministry of Labor - 20 Company Auditing Agency
274 Ministry of Media Affairs - 12.1 Monitoring team

The unedited version must be immediately made available to the Surveillance Television, broadcast and stored on the intranet for public access.

For informer, i.e. humans who uncover corruption and crime, there is immunity from prosecution, even if they themselves were involved. If they were not involved, there is a reward of 10% of the amount of the damage. Informer members receive a statue in the "Garden of Justice" of the Ministry of State Organisation, provided they agree to this.

The People's Protection Service travels around the cities and is supposed to report suspicious objects or occurrences to the Federal Moderator for Internal Affairs. He checks the allegations and files charges if they turn out to be true.

12.2 Immunity[275]

Politicians enjoy immunity to guarantee the freedom of their speech in such a way that they can suggest content that is still a criminal offence. Their immunity only applies to statements made in the legislative process. The aim is to be allowed to raise matters that are punishable and to have them negotiated and voted on in an ordinary legislative process with affected citizens or politicians. This immunity also applies to citizens while they are participating in the above-mentioned legislative process.

There is no immunity from criminal or civil law proceedings for unlawful acts. Unlawful acts by politicians in office are subject to official liability. Politicians are liable with their office and can be held accountable for damage to the people. They are personally liable with their assets or liberty for wilful disregard of applicable laws committed in the course of their activities in state service.

275§67 Immunity: BV Art.162

12.3 Popular empowerment[276]

The people have the right to take control of any ministry at any time, including ministries administered municipally. This occurs when a majority of 60% of the people cast their vote for the empowerment quorum. All deselection quorums of politicians in the affected ministry are automatically triggered. All elected offices are re-elected, re-election of incumbent politicians is not possible. Exceptions to re-election may be voted on by a majority of the committee. All ongoing veto quorums are automatically triggered and all ongoing legislative processes are stopped. The empowerment quorum specifies whether it is individual employees or all employees of one or more ministries.

Popular empowerment is always justified when the will of the people is violated. This is the case as soon as a ministry violates laws or elected politicians in cooperation violate their election programmes and the deselection quorum of a politician is not sufficient to avert this state of affairs.

The Ministry of State Organisation convenes a committee once the empowerment quorum has been triggered. At this committee, it is necessary to clarify which employees are to be dismissed and by whom the state services are to be guaranteed until new personnel are determined. It must also be clarified whether the committee will select the new staff through an election of persons process or whether politicians will be elected to appoint new staff on their own authority. If elected politicians are removed from office, a new election must be held immediately for the corresponding positions. Within the framework of the committee, it is necessary to clarify which official functions must be continued and how this is to be done. For this purpose, past service instructions are consulted that were valid in a period when the ministry had not yet violated the will of the people.

If the Ministry of State Organisation itself is affected by an empowerment quorum and the state service cannot be suspended until the new personnel are in office, citizens who work in disaster management take over. They perform

---

276§68 Popular empowerment, §161,4,5 Financial and burden equalisation their duties to the best of their knowledge and abide by the service instructions issued in the committee as temporarily lawful. Federal Moderators take over the moderation of the committees. If they are declared biased by 10% of those entitled to vote, each committee elects its moderators from among the citizens who report themselves voluntarily to do so. Once new staff have been elected, the citizen volunteers hand over their duties to these persons.

Personnel removed from office by a committee may not be reinstated, receive a lifetime occupational ban from all state service and are expelled from all political parties. All responsible politicians and ministry staff receive criminal proceedings on suspicion of wilful disregard for the will of the people.[277]

New personnel are put to the election by the party of the affected ministry to the citizens or appointed by newly elected politicians of the ministry.

12.4 Protests

When citizens gather to protest against a policy, this is permissible in the context of a demonstration. If citizens gather for regular demonstrations to protest against certain government decisions or politicians, this is considered a protest. Usually, demonstrations are accompanied by solution finding with the People's Motor Vehicle or committees are convened. If responsible politicians fail to properly engage citizens, they are responsible for the protest. Once the Federal Moderator's Office recognises a protest, it is obliged to appoint a People's Motor Vehicle for solution finding at each final rally of protest marches and to moderate the committee, regardless of which ministry would actually be responsible.

If violence against persons or objects occurs during the protests, it is considered rioting[278] . Security personnel will initiate the appropriate procedures to ensure public order.[279] The rioters are first asked by the police to demonstrate peacefully and to participate in a committee. If repeated offences are

277 Ministry of Justice - 8.14.2.2 Disregard for the will of the people
278 Ministry of Security - 7.10 Riot
279 Ministry of Security - 4.9 Demonstrations

committed, rioters are arrested by the police. Participants in the demonstration and passers-by are entitled to detain rioters temporarily until the police arrive. Rioters will be brought before the courts.[280] If police violence is used against peaceful demonstrators, charges can be brought against security agencies by those affected or witnesses.[281]

12.4.1 Support vote

To find out whether a majority or a minority protests, a support vote is held. Those entitled to vote are the people. It is evaluated where how many citizens voted for or against the protest. The support vote can be triggered by citizens through a veto quorum and directly scheduled by the responsible politician. The support vote is possible as a snap vote or regular one-week voting. Whenever the protest is reported in the Government Television, citizens can participate in the flash vote via their People's Computer. Multiple voting is not possible. This gives the people and the responsible politician a picture of the mood. Because not all citizens can watch the committee broadcast at the same time, a regular voting must be held. The vote for this voting can be cast for one week at the voting computer in the town hall.

12.4.2 Protesting minority

If a majority in the population is against the demands of the protest movement, solutions are sought in the committee. The solutions can be the establishment of a cultural protection area, municipal laws or special laws for this individual case, provided the necessary majority is reached in a voting. The aim is to prevent a minority from terrorising the majority in order to impose minority interests on the majority.

---

280 Ministry of Justice - 8.13.7 Riot
281 Ministry of Security - 4.4 Charges against security agencies

12.4.3 Protesting majority

If a majority of the population is in favour of the demands of the protest movement, committees will be held at the site of the protest as long as the protests continue. The Federal Moderator's Office is authorised to use all available People's Motor Vehicles. The aim of the committees is to investigate which politicians are to blame for the current state of affairs. A committee of enquiry is immediately set up against the affected politicians and they are required to attend. For the duration of these committees of enquiry, arrest warrants are issued against affected politicians, with the period of detention corresponding to the duration of a committee meeting. The affected politicians are wanted on international arrest warrants and are brought to the location of the committee by the police immediately after their arrest. If more than one committee is active, it is necessary to go to the nearest location. Affected politicians remain at the location of the committee and spend the rest of the time in pre-trial detention at the local police station. This detention is only permitted if the committee meeting has to be continued the following day. Committee meetings in a state of emergency with compulsory attendance of affected politicians must be suspended for 8 hours within a 24-hour period. The use of the People's Computer during pre-trial detention remains fully permitted for affected politicians. In the case of multiple committees accusing the same politicians but taking place simultaneously in other parts of the country, video conferencing must be established. The Ministry of Media Affairs sets up switching calls between the People's Motor Vehicle and also broadcasts them simultaneously in the committee programme in the Government Television.

12.5 Punitive measures for politicians[282]

Punitive measures for politicians become effective in the dynamic media democracy through various mechanisms. Any citizen can report observed transgressions by politicians. The measures that follow range from reporting the misconduct

---

282 §67.5 Immunity

and an increase in the deselection quorum to a fine or imprisonment.

12.5.1 Open Leaks

Any citizen can anonymously report a politician's wrong decisions, corruption, inaction, violation of the law or breach of words on the Open Leaks intranet portal[283] . Open Leaks also has a computer programme that lists all reported wrong decisions by politicians and checks whether the facts are sufficient for civil or criminal law charges. All detected violations are automatically reported to the Internal Service of the Federal Moderator's Office, which is obliged to check the reports and initiate the appropriate procedure. Incriminating entries about a politician in Open Leaks can lead to a committee of enquiry, new elections, degradation or disempowerment of a politician.

12.5.2 Committee of enquiry[284]

The heads of the audit services[285] are responsible for convening a committee of enquiry. The people may also convene a committee of enquiry with a veto quorum against the alleged unlawful act.

The committee of enquiry is convened as soon as politicians in the state service are alleged to have violated the law or the will of the people and a complaint is filed against them. Citizens can file a complaint with the police or via an entry in Open Leaks.

Thematically, this committee is concerned with where which faults were committed by whom and when, how they can be rectified and avoided in the future. Therefore, the committee of enquiry is divided into two parts. Committees of enquiry are accompanied by the Surveillance Television with numerous inspection visits to all areas of accountability of the affected

---

283 Ministry of Digital Affairs - 14.4 Open Leaks
284 §97 Investigation Committee: BV Art.153
285 Ministries of Media, Security, Justice, Finance, State Organisation - 2.1.2.1 Audit services

politician's ministry. The Surveillance Television organises the committee of enquiry as a show.[286]

The committee of enquiry is an alternative to mere deselection by quorum. This enables the people to find out at any time which politician is responsible for a decision or a circumstance. This is the only way that citizens can put their cross for the deselection quorum with the right politician even in difficult cases of intertwined responsibilities in the event of dissatisfaction.

12.5.2.1 Judgment

The first part serves to determine the verdict. It is determined by the Ministry of Justice and identifies evidence and defendants.[287] Witnesses are called to give testimony and evidence is collected that incriminates or approves accused politicians. The aim of this section is to find out where which faults were committed by whom and when, and to reach a verdict.

The panel includes a judge from the responsible Remit Court and the National Court of Justice, accused politicians and their aides, a lawyer for the accused politician, affected persons and a public prosecutor. At times, the responsible ministers are also on the panel to explain the ministry's working methods, as well as scientists who examine the psyche and socialisation of the offender and the victim in order to present motives, and witnesses who present their statements as evidence. The procedure is equivalent to court proceedings before the National Court of Justice for the taking of evidence and indictment.

12.5.2.2 Solution Finding

The second part is for solution finding. It is determined by the Ministry of State Organisation and corresponds to the procedure of legislative committees. Affected people, party

286Ministry of Media Affairs - 12.3.4.1 Committee of enquiry
287Ministry of Justice - 5.4.5.2 Committee of enquiry

members, experts, ministry staff and citizens look for solutions as to how faults that have been committed can be remedied and avoided in the future.

On the panel are only responsible employees of the affected ministry, scientists and those affected. In accordance with the TV show format "Solution Finder"[288] proposals are sought, discussed, rejected or accepted that will ensure that damage is repaired and that such things do not happen again. Proposals to be introduced as laws are prepared as templates and put to a vote of the people.

12.5.3 New elections

In the dynamic media democracy, new elections are held as soon as the deselection quorum is met. Politicians who make wrong decisions are punished by dissatisfied citizens through the deselection quorum. Thus, after the election, an elected politician is responsible for the entire people or citizens affected by his policies, and not just for his constituents. Once enough citizens have become so dissatisfied during the politician's term of office that they have become involved in the politician's deselection quorum, the deselection quorum is triggered and the post is re-elected. The majority is dependent on the majority that was needed to elect the politician to office.

12.5.4 Degradation

Negligently wrong decisions by politicians that cause financial, material or psychological damage to the population are prosecuted under civil law. Any citizen can file a complaint with the Federal Moderator or on the intranet portal "Open Leaks". The Federal Moderator then decides whether to hold a committee of enquiry against the politician or to file a complaint with the responsible Remit Court as a civil class action. The verdict or the voting at the end of the committee of enquiry decides whether the politician is dismissed and his

---

288 Ministry of Media Affairs - 7.2.3.5 Solution Finder (Legislation Committee)

or her post re-elected. The politician may stand for election again.

12.5.5 Disempowerment

Deliberately wrong decisions by politicians that serve a criminal background, such as corruption, are immediately prosecuted under criminal law. There is no amnesty for politicians in office. Any citizen can file a complaint on the intranet portal "Open Leaks", with the police or the public prosecutor's office. If the court proceedings end in a guilty verdict, the politician is immediately dismissed and new elections are held. The convicted politician may not newly stand for election and must serve his fine or imprisonment. Until the new election, a Federal Moderator takes charge of the ministry and must coordinate all government decisions with the Council of Ministers. The representative legislative process applies should laws be unavoidable during the transition period.

12.6 State of exception[289]

A state of exception is declared when there is no sufficient legal basis for a state of affairs and any further delay would endanger the life and limb of citizens or disproportionately increase the damage. The Minister of State Organisation and his deputies, the mayors, are responsible for declaring a state of exception. All laws enacted under the state of exception are considered urgent laws with the corresponding deadlines and procedures for citizens to vote on them.

If laws need to be enacted immediately, all 18 ministers meet in the Council of Exception. The ministers are allowed to develop draft laws together or submit their own templates and vote on them. A majority of 10 ministers is required for voting. Counter-proposals are not possible.

If laws have to be enacted within 7 days, the representative way of legislating and voting is chosen. Ministers and councillors are entitled to vote and can submit drafts or templates and

---

289§82 State of exception

vote on them. A majority of 55% of those entitled to vote applies.

12.7 State of emergency[290]

A state of emergency is declared whenever citizens or the state have to act in self-defence to protect themselves or other persons from third parties or dangers. The Ministry of Security is responsible for natural hazards and crime.[291] The Ministry of State Organisation is responsible for human-made dangers that endanger the state. Fundamental rights can be restricted in the defence against these dangers. Citizens and state employees are then usually entitled to carry out punishable acts and remain unpunished. These acts are described in the following chapters. Should the security agencies inflict damage on peaceful humans, those affected can file charges against security agencies.[292]

A national or municipal state of emergency is declared when the whole country or a whole municipality is threatened politically and thus also the constitution. Attacks on the basic constitutional order, which may be repelled by force of arms and the restriction of fundamental rights, differ according to the respective opponents. A state of emergency is always declared in the event of war, civil war, coup d'état or coup d'état.

12.7.1 New election in a state of emergency

At a committee in a state of emergency, it may be decided to repeat deselection quorums in public. In this case, the secrecy of the ballot is lifted. All citizens are obliged to cast their vote for the public quorum with compulsory voting within 2 days. The status of the current quorum will be cancelled and set to zero. After the compulsory quorum vote, a new election will

---

290§172 Internal and external security in a state of emergency: KV Art. 91
291 Ministry of Security - 5 Prevention of danger, 6 People's Protection Service, 7 Police, 8 Customs
292 Ministry of Security - 4.4 Charges against security agencies

be held if at least 51% vote in favour. Politicians who have been deselected in such a compulsory vote may not stand for re-election.

12.7.2 Reporting in a state of emergency

In a state of emergency, citizens take over 30% of the broadcasting time in the daily news. All citizens are asked to film persons who are suspected of unlawful behaviour with their own devices and to publish this footage on the citizens' television intranet portal[293] . All published videos will be examined by an algorithm. The same persons and the same places are listed and the highest frequency is shown in the daily news. Persons who commit an offence several times in different places and in the presence of many filmers are shown. Citizens have the right to claim up to 90% of all broadcasters' airtime after a veto quorum, committee and voting. Videos created by citizens that serve to document state or civilian failures will be shown. Each video will have the filmmaker's name at the bottom of the frame. If filmmakers decide against this naming, they can indicate this in advance. In that case, the police will come to them and assure themselves of the authenticity of the footage. The recordings of an anonymous filmmaker are given a number that remains the same for that filmmaker. A statistic shows the viewers how many persons have submitted videos, which persons do so continuously or repeatedly and which of these persons make it into the daily news with their videos and how often. The aim is to identify one-sided reporting.

12.7.3 War

When states fight against states, that is war. The Ministry of Security issues laws that regularise the deployment and equipment of the military.[294] The commander-in-chief of the military must be directly elected by the people. His conduct

293 Ministry of Media - 11 Nationwide Citizen Television
294 Ministry of Security - 9.5 Warfare, 9.4.2 Weapon Systems, 9.4.1 Basic Training, 9.4 Soldiers, 9.3.1 Continental Defence Army

of the war is controlled by the people and can be changed or stopped by a veto quorum. The aim is to defend the inland and the law applicable there. The war ends as soon as a state or an alliance of states surrenders. The national state of emergency is then lifted and all prisoners of war are exchanged.

12.7.4 Civil war

When citizens fight citizens, it is civil war. The Ministry of Security issues laws that regularisation the deployment and equipment of the police.[295] The deputy security ministers of each municipality have the right to call in the military to help break up riots, conduct a city raid or fight the mafia. The aim is to reconcile hostile groups of citizens and arrest criminals. The reconciliation of hostile groups is carried out in specially created situations such as mediation cells, duels and brawls. State organisation ministers or mayors may declare a state of civil war and hold reconciliation committees where groups of citizens discuss their differences and develop compromises.

12.7.5 Revolt

When citizens fight against the state because they oppose government decisions and want to force the government to give in or step down through rioting or terror, it is considered a revolt. A revolt is carried out without firearms by rioting citizens and does not have to have leaders. If there are leaders or ideological targets, the procedure for Mafia Combat and Terrorism applies.[296] If there are no leaders or targets, the procedure for rioting applies.[297] A riot includes the erection of barricades and the storming, occupation and cordoning off of civil or state buildings.

The Ministry of Security issues laws that regularisation the deployment and equipment of the police. The national security minister, as an elected politician, is responsible for

---

295 Ministry of Security - 7.11 Fighting Mafia, 7.10 Riot, 7.12 City raids, 6.6 Dispute resolution
296 Ministry of Security - 4.11 Terrorism, 7.11 Fighting the Mafia
297 Ministry of Security - 7.10 Riot, 4.9.1 Violent demonstrations

combating revolts. The police investigate terrorist or mafia unifications and rioters at home and abroad. The Ministry of Foreign Affairs provides international police agreements and information from the embassies. The police apprehend terrorists or rioters during or shortly before their crime, if possible, or at the latest afterwards. They have the right to call in the military for support.

It hands over violent citizens to the justice system[298] and leads violent and frustrated citizens to the committees of the Ministry of State Organisation. Detained citizens are obliged to participate in committees via videoconference from prison to express their motives. Citizens in pre-trial detention continue to have voting rights. Convicted citizens have no voting rights for interactive proceedings, only for voting.

Once the police have identified suspects, they hand over the personal data to the Federal Moderator's Office. Moderators attempt to contact suspects to inquire about dissatisfactions and invite them to participate in appropriate quorums, committees or party work.

The aim of these committees is to inquire into the political causes of the citizens' discontent and to develop solutions that are in accordance with the applicable law. The possibilities of popular empowerment, the committee of enquiry, charges against security agencies, petition or initiative, and the creation of a cultural protection area are examined and applied as appropriate. Attention is drawn to the possibility of casting a vote at any time, for the affected quorum of the law, constitutional article or politician.

12.7.6 Coup

When citizens fight against the state with the aim of usurping the government of one, several or all ministries, without using the applicable electoral procedure, this is a coup. For a coup, there must be leaders and organised forces.[299] Action against coup d'étatists is the same as against insurgents in a coup d'état, because it makes no difference in terms of measures

---

298 Ministry of Justice - 8.14.5.2 Revolt
299 Ministry of Justice - 8.14.5.3 Coup

whether the persons are in the state service or not. The coup can be national or municipal by force of arms or digital. The procedures apply accordingly, as in the respective coup d'état.

12.7.7 Coup d'état[300]

When the state fights against its citizens, it is a coup d'état. It either means that the security minister as commander-in-chief of the military, the deputy or municipal security minister has abused his office or has been forcibly removed from office and another person or group of persons has taken or wants to take the monopoly of violence away from the people's supreme command. Or it means that voting results have been manipulated or voters have been misinformed or deceived in order to take or retain power in the state.[301] In this case, the digital minister or administrators may abuse the office or be unlawfully removed from office and another person or group of persons may violate data security.

A coup d'état can be municipal or national by force of arms or by electoral manipulation. The Ministry of State Organisation issues laws that regularise the actions and rights of citizens and responsible politicians in the event of a coup d'état. The Minister of State Organisation or their deputies in the municipalities, the mayors, take charge of the country or their municipality during the coup d'état, following this and the following laws on coup d'état. Legislative and election of persons processes are suspended during a coup d'état. However, if urgent laws are to be enacted, a state of exception must be declared and the Council of Exceptions shall advise and vote on the bill.

---

300 §172 Internal and external security in a state of emergency: KV Art. 91
301 Ministry of Justice - 8.14.5.4 Coup d'état

12.7.7.1 Proclamation of the coup d'état

Anyone who recognises a coup d'état must immediately inform the nearest mayor or the police. The police inform the mayor. The mayors inform each other, the state organisation minister, the local public prosecutor's office and the local police. All state organs check the report and report back within 60 minutes. If there is a coup d'état, the mayors of all municipalities declare a state of emergency and take the prescribed measures together with the local population.

12.7.7.2 Coup d'état by force of arms

As soon as a person or group of persons from the Ministry of Security wants to seize the leadership of the state or a municipality by force of arms, this is considered a coup d'état by force of arms. These persons are hereafter called insurgents. A person or group of persons who was able to place all or part of the armed personnel of the Ministry of Security, their weapons and devices under their command, is considered to be the leader of the coup d'état by force of arms. The same applies if arms or persons, are not part of the equipment or personnel of the Ministry of Security, i.e. in a coup. Any employees of the Ministry of Security who are loyal to the Constitution, together with any available material, fight alongside the citizens against the insurgents.

12.7.7.2.1 Municipal responsibility

In the event of a national coup d'état, the national level is suspended during this emergency period. All national ministers and their ministries thus automatically become ineffective. All national ministers flee abroad and meet in a country that grants them asylum. They keep in touch with their deputies as far as possible. Their offices are suspended for the duration of the state of emergency. The municipal level takes over all previously national functions. All municipalities temporarily administer themselves. All deputy ministers temporarily become municipal ministers. All national and international laws temporarily become municipal laws.

The municipalities take the planned measures in the councils of ministers to fight the insurgents nationwide. All municipalities that are not under the control of the insurgents work together in an alliance of municipalities against the insurgents and try to liberate all occupied municipalities. The mayors, as municipal deputies of the Minister of State Organisation, and the deputy ministers of security have the lead responsibility.

12.7.7.2.2 Handling insurgents

Any criminal security forces or armed insurgents who seek to take over the government of the country by force of arms are considered unfree for the duration of the state of emergency. Thus, their violation and detention until they are handed over to the police is not a criminal offence. The abduction and detention of their relatives is permissible for the duration of the state of emergency. Torture and murder remain inadmissible.

12.7.7.2.3 Arming the population

If it is a national, i.e. nationwide coup d'état by force of arms, the state of emergency alarm is triggered with a specific sound signal. The citizens immediately begin to prepare for the rehearsed state of siege. This process is already introduced as a law in peacetime, negotiated with all citizens, voted on and rehearsed every 10 years. All citizens of the municipality have defined tasks for which they have reported voluntarily and are trained. They store all the necessary material at their homes or in the storage facilities of the local rescue services.

The population is armed with weapons from the armouries of the local police stations, as is customary in the event of war. No ammunition will be issued during the exercises. All lethal weapons of war are kept in the armoury of the local police stations and issued to the citizens. Rocket launchers and heavy machine guns are operated by fellow citizens who were good with them during basic training.

12.7.7.2.4 Vigilantes

The citizens form a vigilante group that immediately searches all streets and houses for armed insurgents, disarms them and imprisons or kills them if the insurgents resist with force. In all municipalities, citizens erect barricades around the town hall with their vehicles, block all access roads and set up checkpoints on access roads. If telecommunications are disrupted, the municipalities communicate with smoke signals, smoke grenades, flare guns, sound signals or ambassadors and scouts. The communication languages and signs are listed in a manual. In the event of war, new manuals are also issued to use an unknown type of encryption.
Some of the vigilantes are deployed with the armed forces to counterattack. The remaining members of the vigilante remain in the municipality, securing the outer borders through checkpoints and patrolling the town.

12.7.7.2.5 Counterattack

After the municipality has been secured, the counterattack is organised. Once the municipality is free of insurgents, another signal is sounded. The vigilante sends its designated members as forces and converts suitable vehicles and aircraft from the municipality to fight. All municipalities dispatch their forces, which assemble where insurgents are still oppressing citizens or occupying buildings. Once the municipalities have dispatched all designated combat units and these forces have assembled in front of the insurgents' location, the siege perimeters of vehicles and barricades are drawn closer and closer around that location. Insurgents' vehicles and aircraft are destroyed and buildings they are in are stormed or set on fire. If possible, the insurgents are disarmed, tied up and imprisoned. If they resist, they will be injured or killed if necessary. If a storming would cause many civilian casualties, the state of siege will be maintained until the insurgents run out of food.

12.7.7.2.6 Surrender

Municipalities can surrender once 65% of the citizens of that municipality have given their consent. The approval is given through a quorum. For this purpose, a ballot box is placed in each town hall during the coup d'état. Citizens have to throw their passports into the ballot box if they want to surrender. On the sealed ballot box there is a counter that turns over as soon as a passport is thrown in. Next to the counter is the number of votes needed to reach the quorum. As soon as this number is reached, all citizens are asked to pick up their passports. In the presence of everyone, the ballot box is opened, everyone receives their passports and the count is newly conducted. If the number is not correct, the ballot box is put back in place. If the majority of 65% is reached, all weapons of war must be surrendered to a municipality that has not surrendered. If this is not possible, the weapons must be destroyed in a designated place in a previously practised procedure. Following the destruction or transfer of the weapons, the mayor reports the surrender of that municipality. A white flag is hoisted on the town hall and all checkpoints.

12.7.7.3 Municipal coup d'état by force of arms

If a person or group of persons is in command of armed forces of the Ministry of Security and thus attempts to gain control of a municipality, this is considered a municipal coup d'état by force of arms. The Ministry of Security, through the other security forces in the country, namely the police and the military, ensures that insurgents are disarmed and arrested and only killed if necessary. The procedure corresponds to the defence against a coup, because it is irrelevant whether persons or groups of persons are state employees or not.[302] If necessary, the population is armed and vigilante forces are sent in to support the other security forces.

---

302 Ministry of Security - 9.5.2 Coup

12.7.7.3.1 National responsibility

In the case of a coup d'état, the affected municipality is administered centrally for the duration of the coup. All municipal politicians are bound by the instructions of the national minister. Failure to comply with these instructions is considered complicity in the coup d'état and is punishable by occupational ban and imprisonment. The nation takes the designated measures to recapture the insurgent municipality and fight insurgents.

12.7.7.4 Digital coup d'état through election manipulation

As soon as a person or group of persons in one or more ministries or municipalities restricts the democratic rights of citizens through digital manipulation, election manipulation or an act of sabotage on the intranet, this is considered a digital coup d'état. The search for those responsible is made possible for every citizen by publishing all data on voter behaviour of the affected voting. The police will form the state search team. Insurgents involved will be brought to justice.[303]

Data manipulation is permanently detected by a programme. All deviations from the norms are detected and reported by the system. The alarm message is sent to the External Service of the Federal Moderator's Office, the Institute for Information Security[304] and the Digital Police[305] .

12.7.7.4.1 Control mechanisms

As a digital control mechanism, a piece of software for subsequent correction, a So-called patch, or one of the existing reserve operating systems is installed as a new operating system on all voting computers. The voting is repeated digitally.

As an analogue control mechanism, the electoral rolls are published in the town hall. The secrecy of the ballot is broken and all citizens are supposed to control their voting behaviour

303 Ministry of Justice - 8.14.5.4 Coup d'état
304 Ministry of Digital Affairs - 8 Digital Crime
305 Ministry of Security - 7.7 Digital Police

in the list. Those who voted differently, or who actually did not vote at all, report this. As soon as the voter has controlled his or her own field, this field on voting behaviour is blacked out and is no longer visible to other controlling voters. Only the name and whether voting has taken place is displayed. All fields that are not blacked out after one week will be contacted by the Federal Moderator's Office and questioned in person. If the suspicion of manipulated voting is confirmed, this voting will be repeated analogously.

12.7.7.4.2 Analogue election

During the analogue repetition of the voting, the secrecy of the ballot is lifted. The voting and counting of the votes takes place simultaneously in public and is broadcast on state television. Citizens go to a public square where an area is cordoned off. Once all citizens are present, they enter the cordoned-off area through two turnstiles each. There are two turnstiles with mechanical counters at each passage. One turnstile is red and stands for "No". The other is green and stands for "Yes". A camera continuously films the run-through of the persons and the jumping over of the counter. Passers-through can watch the counter jumping around by themselves and other participants. In order to run-through the turnstile, one's passport must be handed over to a police officer who stands at the turnstile and collects and stamps passports. Once all participating citizens have gathered in the cordoned-off area, voting ends and the result is announced on state television. Local participants check the visible count on the turnstiles and on the list of turnstiles on state television. If a difference is detected, observers can announce this at the public microphone, which must be placed next to each counter display. When the audience microphone is activated, a camera is automatically pointed at the speaker and goes on the air. After all the counters have been totalled, the voting is considered over and the voters receive their passports back.

12.7.7.4.3 Manipulation of opinion

In the case of election manipulation through opinion manipulation on the intranet, authors of affected contributions are forced to add a counterstatement to their contribution, because otherwise the contribution will be deleted and a monetary fine must be paid for its further dissemination.

Contributions that manipulate opinion are designed in such a way that they only report negatively, derogatorily and badly about a matter without presenting their own proposal for a solution. Contributions on the intranet should not only contain criticism, but also statements or proposals as to how the author would like things to be in his/her opinion. In committees, only persons are allowed to publish or rate contributions and comments. In other areas of the intranet, profiles of companies and associations also have this right. Persons may not be forced by companies or associations to publish content in their name.

The search for the responsible persons is started by reports from other users to the digital police station. The police have the right to retrieve the publication of all the suspect's data on the intranet. If there are violations, the data set is handed over as evidence to the responsible public prosecutor's office and court proceedings are initiated for opinion manipulation.[306]

12.7.7.5 End of the coup d'état

The coup d'état ends when all insurgents have been imprisoned or killed in action. It also ends when all the municipalities have surrendered.

After the coup d'état, committees must investigate the opinions and motivations of the opponents and find solutions in negotiations. The Ministry of State Organisation is responsible for these committees.

After an averted coup d'état, the insurgents are sentenced in court proceedings[307] which are broadcast on state television. The court proceedings are accompanied by committees in

---

306 Ministry of Justice - 8.10.4 Manipulation of opinion on the intranet
307 Ministry of Justice - 8.14.5.4 Coup d'état

which faults and successes are discussed. This is done with the aim of enacting laws, if necessary, to improve procedural rules during a coup d'état. The ministers in exile return and resume their work.

13 Switching to the new system

The new system requires reforms of political structures and processes. In future, persons and laws will be directly elected. For each ministry there is a remit party and a capital city.

13.1 Amendment of the constitution[308]

The fundamental changes will be determined by the people through the dismantling of the existing constitution and the simultaneous construction of a new constitution. As a template for the new constitution, the constitution of the dynamic media democracy will be brought in. To make the concrete implementation easier to understand, the constitution of the Swiss Confederation and the constitution of the Canton of Bern are used as aids.

Titles 2 to 4 on state organisation, state powers and federalism are dealt with first. All articles are negotiated one after the other in a constitutional committee and the corresponding articles of the old constitution are replaced by them. At the end of each chapter there is a voting on it. Once all chapters have been voted on at least once, the entire new constitution is put to a vote. Only this voting is compulsory. If it is adopted, the old constitution loses its validity. In this last act, the new constitution comes into force if 80% of the nationals living inland give their consent. The entire constitution-making process may not take longer than 4 years. The implementation takes place on the internet because there is no intranet yet. A page for the Constitutional Court will be created on the Constitutional Court's website. Through this page, citizens can register with their identity card and express, comment on and rate suggestions for improving the constitution.

---

308 §261 Transitional provision towards this Constitution

Contributions with high ratings will be discussed in the Constitutional Committee. The Constitutional Committee is broadcast in real time by state television and held in the spirit of the "Solution Finder" show concept.[309] At the committee meetings, the articles of the new constitution are drafted into templates. Once all the articles of a chapter have been drafted, the people vote on them. An election week is scheduled for each chapter and each chapter must be filmed and shown on state television. Before the final vote on the entire constitution, all films on the chapters must be newly shown. The broadcast shall be in prime time in the week preceding the election week. The film must be permanently viewable on the state television website no later than after the broadcast. During film scenes based on a passage of a constitutional article, the relevant passage shall be displayed at the bottom of the screen. In order to be able to hold the constitutional referendum without an intranet, the data from the voting computers is reported and merged via the private and state media. The Chief Electoral Officer performs the aggregation as an employee of the Ministry of State Organisation. State television, free media representatives and international election observers monitor the voting on the chapters and in particular the final constitutional referendum after which the new constitution comes into force. Otherwise, the constitution-making process takes place like a constitutional amendment through a total revision.

13.2 Similarities with the dynamic media democracy

One can imagine democratic countries in their current state as fully parliamentarised. It is as if the people in the dynamic media democracy had decided, after a participation quorum, to have the election and legislation done by councils. For the individual ministries, it is as if all the municipalities had chosen certain ministries to be governed by municipalities. All the municipalities would have come together within the

---

309	Ministry of Media Affairs - 7.2.3.5 Solution Finder (Legislation Committee)

boundaries of today's regions and decided to govern certain ministries in an alliance of municipalities. All nationals would have decided to have certain ministries governed nationally within the national borders. All citizens would have chosen to lend out their votes to one party wing at the national, regional and municipal levels of government.

In the current legislation, however, many ministries are active at several political levels. For the Ministry of State Organisation, the first task is to distribute the competences of nation, region and municipality to the new political levels for international, national or municipal responsibility.

13.3 Introduction of the 18 ministries

If the party that wants to introduce this system obtains an absolute majority and forms the government alone, it fills all ministries with its own interim ministers. Then the government distributes all the responsibilities of the ministries into the 18 ministries of this system. Unnecessary ministries are closed and new ministries are opened. Transitional ministers change ministries or are newly appointed by the government. The transitional ministers take care of the move of the departments. During the transition period, all national ministries are still located in the country's capital city. Until the new buildings are ready for occupancy, work is done in the old buildings.

Once the regions have been abolished, the ministries move into buildings in their respective capital cities. The Federal Moderator's Office replaces the Office for the Head of State.

Departments for state, constitutional and administrative law from the Ministry of the Interior are continued in the Ministry of State Organisation.

Once all responsibilities have been redistributed and all departments have been moved, ministers will be elected directly one by one. The minimum interval between these elections of persons must be at least 2 months to allow each minister to present his or her programme. The party that has introduced this system will contest with the election programme described in the respective volume for the ministry. Once all

18 Ministers are directly elected, the Head of Government becomes the Federal Moderator for Politicians and the leader of the Internal Service of the Federal Moderator's Office. The President becomes the Federal Moderator for Citizens and Leader of the External Service of the Federal Moderator's Office. Both Federal Moderators receive a deselection quorum when they change office. The quorum is triggered once 50% of the people are in favour. In the run-off election, a majority must vote for one candidate.

13.4 Reform of the party system

The old parties have always had working groups categorised by remit in their internal structure. In the new system, there are 18 ministries covering all the remits where policy is made. Therefore, there is one party for each ministry. Therefore, one can speak of 18 remit parties here. To make political competition possible, each party has any number of party wings. The old parties are placed in these party wings.

In this way, a smooth transition can be achieved. 18 parties are established. What is new is that one may be a member of any number of the 18 parties. Only an expertise or interest in the remit is expected.

Each existing party is required to form 18 remits with corresponding working groups by a deadline. If this is not possible for a party, it cannot stand for election for that ministry. All working groups of the parties assign themselves to their corresponding remit party and establish a party wing there with the name of their old party. In all remit parties there are thus initially all parties that deal with the remit in their party programme and have working groups for it. Each party wing bears the name of the old party. Therefore, in the beginning all party wings in all parties are called the same. Later, they will have names that have more to do with the remit and the ways of resolving issues. During the transition period, wings can be renamed, dissolved or newly created. A new wing must consist of at least 3 persons and be programmatically different from the other wings. Party members are free to change wings from proposal to proposal. Party wings prepare programmes and proposals. They submit proposals to the incumbent minister and work out programmes for election campaigns.

All those entitled to vote nationals lend out their votes to one party wing per remit party. To do so, they must choose an existing party for each of the 18 ministries. All existing parties structure their programmes by department so that those entitled to vote need only read the affected chapter to make their choice.

The new parties are sorted by remit. Anyone can remain a member of their old party for the time being and simply join one or more remit parties as a member. At the beginning, party members wear their party's logo as a badge when they meet as remit parties. At the beginning, each old party represents a wing in the remit parties. This makes it clearer in which direction their proposed solutions could go.

13.4.1 Coalitions

Until now, after the election, parties looked for common ground in their programmes, exchanged proposals in order to be able to implement certain proposals. These coalition negotiations now take place publicly, before the pre-election in the party and after the pre-election in the programme committee. The party wings each make proposals for solutions on how to deal with a task in the ministry. In the party, each member is now allowed to choose a proposed solution and it does not have to be the proposal of their party wing. These coalition negotiations must be broadcast on the internet and on state television. The people can now also rate the proposed solutions themselves. The trade and barter of election promises, now takes place before and after the pre-election and is conducted publicly. As soon as digital participation possibilities are in place, citizens will be involved in the process.

13.5 Location reform

The new capital cities are the capitals of all regions because parliamentary buildings are located there. The work of the councils and party headquarters takes place in the new capital city of the respective ministry. The parties use the former parliamentary buildings to bring their party wings together for coalition negotiations on a particular proposal. The minister always attends these meetings. He decides whether the selection of proposals should be done by the party or by the citizens.

13.5.1 Turning cities, municipalities and counties into municipalities

All town halls that administer a population of less than 5000 inhabitants are merged. All town halls that administer a population of over 10000 inhabitants are considered to have merged several municipalities. Regions are considered to be municipalities that administer several ministries themselves and have merged within the national borders of their region. The population can introduce these states through a subsidiarity quorum. By default, all ministries are administered nationally. The subsidiarity quorum is automatically triggered for the first time when the regions are dissolved.

13.6 Dissolve federal intermediate levels

The intermediate federal levels between municipalities and the nation, So-called regions, federal states or federal states, are abolished. Their buildings for parliaments and ministries will continue to be used. Each ministry gets its own capital city. These are 18 capital cities of the former regions. The people must make a joint choice here as to which city should become the capital city for which ministry. The locations should match the ministry's area of responsibility as much as possible. Remaining buildings are converted into housing or state enterprises or sold. The people must agree to the sale.

13.6.1 Municipal division

The citizens of the regions are allowed to tick additionally in the voting for the dissolution of the regions if they want to vote on it in their own region. Suppose the whole people of the country are in favour of dissolving the regions, but the majority in one region is against it. In that case, the exception rule applies that the municipalities are then administered in the alliance of the region. As a transition, these exceptions should gradually be based only on details, i.e. individual solutions, and no longer take over an entire remit. The question should always be: What can the municipality do better than the whole country? What can the municipality not do as well as the whole country and what can the whole country not do as well as a certain region?

All municipalities with their own town halls become municipalities and can make their own municipal policy. Municipalities are allowed to join together to form districts or regions in order to make jointly coordinated municipal policy, similar to what has been done so far. The former regional parliaments meet on a rotating basis in the largest plenary halls of the town halls if the citizens have opted for a union of municipalities.

The regions could theoretically continue to exist in the new system without any problems. For example, all the municipalities in a region could join together and hold a subsidiarity vote for each ministry that is currently under regional administration. Then all ministers would only have to be directly elected instead of being appointed by a head of government. The office of Head of Government will be replaced by the office of Federal Moderator. For example, when the Council of Ministers of Education is to meet, all municipal education ministers will meet in a plenary hall of one of their town halls, in a stadium or digitally.

13.6.2 Dissolve regional parliaments

A ministry and its party move into the former regional parliaments and buildings of the regional ministries. Other buildings are sold. All members of the regional parliaments are dismissed after the current election period ends and no new elections are held.

The ministries, which were previously administered regionally, get a directly elected minister. Under new state law, ministers, whether at municipal or national level, must always be directly elected. Citizens elect deputy ministers for their municipality, who form the Council of Ministers at the national level.

Citizens will gradually be able to dissolve more and more parliaments and decide for themselves on national or municipal laws and annual budgets, once all the multimedia tools, the ministries of media and digital, are available.

13.7 Reduce parliaments and levels of government

The municipal or local parliament becomes the party council and the national parliament becomes the council of ministers. All other parliaments are abolished and their deputies dismissed. The parliamentary buildings serve as meeting places in the capital cities for the new 18 parties and ministries. All remaining members of parliament will be given a deselection quorum. At the latest after the new constitution comes into force, every member of the local parliament must be a delegate of the relevant party and every member of the national parliament must be a deputy minister of the relevant ministry. To this end, citizens of a municipality elect one delegate per party according to personal preference and one deputy minister per ministry in the election of persons process.

13.7.1 Cabinet reshuffle

The cabinet of the existing government is dissolved after the last legislative period. The last legislative period begins when the new party obtains an absolute majority or forms the government with sufficient votes. Each minister is responsible for his or her own decisions after the last legislative period, once he or she is directly elected and can be directly deselected by quorum. The head of government, as the new Federal Moderator, only chairs cabinet meetings if several ministries are involved in an individual case.

13.7.2 Introduction of the Council of Ministers

For the changeover, the citizens have decided to be represented nationally by a council, i.e. to currently use representative democracy as a form of procedure. To this end, the members of the national parliament become the deputy ministers of the municipalities. At the time of the changeover, the constituencies are larger than the municipalities. The offices for the deputy ministers in the town halls are staffed by clerks who are supported by the members of the national parliament with instructions from their constituency office. The national parliament is initially the place where each council of ministers meets. It is not actually possible to fill more than one ministry, but for the changeover, members of the national parliament are deputy ministers for all the ministries in their constituency. The municipalities gradually elect all 18 deputy ministers.

The party wings must put up candidates. Each municipality is considered a constituency and receives a mandate. For example, candidates would be elected from every constituency across the country from the Education Party. Each constituency decides on the programme of one party wing and elects the candidate to represent that programme. He then becomes a councillor in the Council of Ministers in the capital city and can be re-elected by quorum. Once the process is complete, the parliaments are renamed councils.

The election of persons replaces the parliamentary elections for the nation, region, municipality, city and mayoral elections. The pre-election takes up the election programmes. There are publicly conducted coalition negotiations until the run-off election. In the run-off election, the post is awarded. Once the new posts have been filled and trained, the members of the national, regional and local parliaments are dismissed.

The deputy ministers of the Ministry of State Organisation are the new mayors, and the old mayors are dismissed. To avoid dismissal, incumbent politicians can also stand for the election of persons.

13.7.3 Introduction of the Party Council

As soon as the new parties are functioning and the voting procedures are digitalised, i.e. voting can take place on voting computers in polling booths in town halls, citizens can lend out their votes.

13.7.4 Reshuffle of the parliamentary groups

Depending on the ministry, different governing coalitions become possible. All members of parliament in the national parliament remain elected, but they place themselves in one or more remits according to expertise. Only those parliamentarians who have the relevant knowledge, which they have usually already gained in their party's working groups, were represented in the specialised committees. The parliamentary groups are now separated along party lines and there is no longer factional compulsion. Depending on how many supporters a proposed solution has, the party wings can be larger or smaller and thus more or fewer parliamentarians can be represented in the parliamentary groups. Depending on which ministry is currently debating a proposal in a specialised committee, there are as many parliamentary groups as the ministry's party has wings.

After the transition period, the wings will be sorted according to solutions and no longer according to old party membership. Every citizen who wants to improve something in one or more remit parties joins that remit party and participates in the solution finding. After the transition period, citizens can participate via the intranet and no longer have to belong to a party. Parliamentary groups are formed in the parliamentary group and the council of ministers as soon as these bodies have been introduced.

13.8 Introduction of sliding subsidiarity

There is an agreement between the political levels through the principle of subsidiarity that problems will be solved where they can be solved most effectively. In this way, it will continue to be possible to obtain successful solutions from the regions. For the global success of this policy system, it is necessary to be able to draw boundaries flexibly within the state in matters of life and fact. The smallest unit here is a municipality with at least 5,000 inhabitants, i.e. a village, a district, a large city or a county. These units can join together flexibly, for example to maintain a region as a political level. The country becomes a nation when the people give themselves a constitution. The Continental Union becomes an international Union, with Continental Union candidate countries or neighbouring countries, such as Switzerland, in the outer ring. The Continental Union member states, are also in the outer ring, whereby no ministry is yet administered internationally, but there are already many individual cases where ministries have common laws, i.e. Continental Union regulations, or the same laws, i.e. Continental Union directives, as well as common agencies.

Once the Subsidiarity Agency has been imported, its first activity is to convert the regions to the new federal system. In the process, the regions initially retain their responsibilities within the municipal alliance. Once the process is complete, subsidiarity votes will be held for all areas of accountability of the regions and their parliaments. Once all these votes are completed, the subsidiarity quorum applies.

13.9 Transition of the political processes

In order to be able to import the new political structures and processes, representative democracy is used as the initial setting. This means that the procedures for the election of persons and legislation are set in the representative way.

The incumbent ministers remain in office but are given a deselection quorum. For the legislative process, the representative route is chosen, so that the parliaments are transformed into the councils of the respective level and negotiate on legislative texts. All sessions are streamed simultaneously and uncut by webcam on the parliament's website and then offered as a video for download.

Gradually, the local and regional parliaments are dissolved. The national parliament and the municipal parliaments are transformed into the council of ministers and the municipal party council. Constituencies are transformed into municipalities so that members of the national parliament become deputy ministers. Members of local parliaments become municipal delegates to the municipal party council.

13.9.1 Election workers

As long as the digital election and voting procedures have not yet been imported, election workers will take over this task. To avoid electoral fraud, election workers must be newly selected by lot at each election. Anyone who has once been an election worker is also taken from the lottery drum until it is empty. If there are no more lots in the lottery drum for election workers, it is newly filled up with all residents. Anyone who is demonstrably prevented from voting on an election date may cancel up to 3 times and will be newly entered into the lottery. The lots in the lottery bear numbers assigned to a person in the population register. The procedure for drawing lots takes place in each municipality and must be held in public. The counting of the votes by the election workers is monitored by video and transmitted in real time on the internet. Video surveillance must be uninterrupted from the time the seal is broken until the result of the counting of all ballot papers is announced. Voters must ensure that the ballot box into which they cast their ballot paper is sealed.

13.9.2 Committees and voting

Compared to parliamentarianism, committee meetings are no longer held by a few parliamentarians in the parliament building, but in parliament buildings in the capital cities, mobile TV studios in public places and on the intranet.

Compared to parliamentarism, plenary votes on policy decisions are no longer accepted or rejected by all parliamentarians during the plenary week in the parliament building, but by all affected citizens during the election week in the voting booths of the town halls or by all members of the responsible council.

Committees need a digital infrastructure that has to be provided before committees can meet in a legally secure way. Initially, their process is used in councils to show citizens how the new process works. State television broadcasts these shows in real time. Increasingly, more interactive participation options are introduced for viewers to use.

Voting is held as soon as there is an intranet café complete with voting booths in all town halls. Initially, there is no intranet yet, which is why only the websites are accessible, providing admission to those entitled to vote with information and opportunities to participate in day-to-day political business. After voters have been able to inform themselves sufficiently, they vote in the voting booth during an election week. Until this infrastructure is developed, postal voting replaces voting at the voting computer in the polling booth during the election week.

13.9.3 Introduction of the quorum

The quorums are initially analogue and later digital. For each analogue quorum, a ballot box is placed in the town hall. Votes can only be cast in the town hall where citizens reside. Anyone who casts a vote is removed from the directory for that ballot box. Ministry of State Organisation staff enter each vote into the Quorum's digital profile in the Quorum Directory. Initially, the data is stored in the town hall and sent via the internet to a central computer in the main building of the Ministry of State Organisation. There, the votes from all town halls converge and it automatically detects when a quorum is triggered. The stands of all quorums can be viewed on the Ministry of State Organisation's website.

13.9.4 Reform of the election of persons and legislation

First, the representative way of election of persons and legislative process is taken. All sessions are broadcast on state television to inform the population which procedures they will be able to participate in. In the transition phase, more and more interactive participation options will be introduced. At the beginning, the audience will be involved in all studios of state television. After that, the audience will be involved via an internet app for smartphones. Meetings are then held in the intranet cafés of the town halls when the first committees also meet digitally. The ministries of media and digital ensure representative polls during the televised broadcast of the committees. As soon as People's Computers are available, all those entitled to vote will have all real and digital participation possibilities at their disposal.

13.9.5 Validation of the new digital voting system

As soon as the voting computers are instituted in the town halls, elections are double-counted by ballot paper and voting computer. The results of the votes cast and counted electronically and by hand are compared. Once new digital voting is imported, a 100% match must be achieved in at least three ballots. Any discrepancies shall be justified, audited and rectified.

13.9.6 People's Computer release

The People's Computers will be issued as soon as the Intranet is available across the country and into the town halls as a cable and via the radio masts as a wireless signal and the People's Innovation Company Intranet has produced sufficient People's Computers. Initially, pre-orders are requested from all those who are willing to use the People's Computer. As soon as this number is reached, the computers will be delivered.
People's Computers are able to access the intranet. Initially, only domestic citizens will have admission to the national

intranet. Voting on intranet access for foreigners living inland may only take place once the new constitution has been adopted as a whole by all nationals.

13.10 Labour market restructuring for state servants

As a result of the reformed state service and the reduction of bureaucracy, many state employees will lose their current jobs or move on to other jobs in the state service.

Social work is mainly offered in Social Villages. Social welfare offices are no longer necessary. The Social Village gate arranges all services and settles accounts with the central office in the Ministry of Planned Economy.

Tax Offices are no longer necessary. Taxes are directly deducted through the compulsory account at the People's Bank and transferred to the Ministry of Finance. Tax evasion is investigated by special units in the Ministry of Labour, Ministry of Finance and Ministry of Security[310] . Checks are carried out everywhere inland on a spot check basis and focus on sectors such as the banking industry, large-scale production industry and restaurants.

Tax officials with a lot of experience in auditing companies come to the Company Auditing Agency and are trained to do so in auditing and giving advice to companies and authorities. They track down wasted resources and are expected to promote and improve Social Market Economy & Planned Economy companies.

Advantages can be sought through further training of some tax law specialists towards international tax law. Proposals to improve the legal situation can be discussed with citizens and politicians on committees and, if necessary, decided upon through every innovative thought of a civil servant.

Natural monopolies such as electricity, water, development, research, education go on the state's central job board, where all paid positions to be filled are listed. The potentially unemployed civil servant is free to choose and, in case of

---

310   Ministry of Security - 8.3 Tax Investigation Department, Ministry of Labour - 20.7.1 Tax Auditor, Ministry of Finance - 5 Tax Policy

doubt, to vote with other civil servants.

Civil servants are no longer recruited in their traditional status. State employees have permanent employment contracts. Job cuts are to be made possible through lower numbers of new hires.

13.10.1 Conversion of state service salaries

Salaries no longer increase according to years of life or length of service. The same wage is paid over the entire working life. This age discrimination is outdated in the age of flexible labour markets. Very few people stay with a company for their entire working life. And if they do, it should not be for the money. In addition, the performance bonus will be introduced as soon as the Ministry of Labour has imported the bonus-malus system.

13.11 Restructuring in the office for the head of government

The office for the Head of Government becomes the Ministry of State Organisation. The Minister of State Organisation replaces the Head of Government. The departments of the Office for the Head of Government are aligned with the new ministries. The State Department maintains sub-departments for ministries, which often work together. The department for the secret services goes to the Ministry of Security.

13.12 Conversion of the old ministries

For the conversion of the old ministries, all departments and units of the old ministries that are changing to this ministry are identified. The organigrams are used to determine whether an entire department and all its units are changing or only individual units. All unsuitable departments and units are dropped. The existing staff adapts its tasks to the new requirements.

Contact form

Dear reader
If you would like to make what you have read come true, in whole or in part, together with other like-minded people, I offer you several possibilities with this contact form. Fill it out, tear out the page and send it by post to:
Andreas Seidl, P.O. Box 1206, 63488 Seligenstadt / Germany

Or send the details to:
Phone: 0049 1522 818 2243 (whatsapp, telegram, signal)
Email: andreas.seidl2022@web.de

Please mark with a cross:
O   I want to found a dynamic People's Party.
O   I want to donate money for implementation.
O   I want contacts with like-minded people in my area.

Forename: _______________________________________

Surname: _______________________________________

Please fill in only the contact option through which a reply should be made.

Street, house no.:   _______________________________

Postcode, city, country: _______________________________

Phone: _______________________________

Email address: _______________________________